Me and You and the People in the Pews

TRACY MOORE

ISBN: 1500463108
ISBN-13: 978-1500463106

Cover design: Chad Landman
Interior graphics and layout: Joey Sparks
Professional editing: Kathy Jarrell

Published by The Jenkins Institute

TheJenkinsInstitute.com

DEDICATION

To my melancholy/phlegmatic wife, Missy. It was her outer beauty that caught my eye, but it was her personality that captured my heart. She has given me four great children, Lex, Noah, Micah and Bella, that have filled our home with the joys of every temperament type. Thank you for believing in me.

CONTENTS

A NOTE TO TEACHERS OR GROUP LEADERS:

This book is made up of 12 chapters (Introduction + 11 chapters) and most quarters last 13 weeks. I recommend, if you can, using the first class for everyone to take the personality test developed by Florence Littauer. It is composed of 40 questions, and it will likely take up a class period.

You can purchase these at http://classervices.com. Under the "Online Store" tab, choose "Personality Resources," and select the "Wired That Way Assessment Tool." They start at $2 each, but cost less for certain quantities. I recommend it because it is very detailed, provides definitions and detailed explanations of scores and the chart.

FOREWARD

Tracy gave me the manuscript to the book you have in front of you over 10 years ago. I put it in the trunk of my car and kept meaning to read it. I would see it when I had a flat or when I was looking for something. Eventually I traded cars, it made its way into a box. All I could do was recommend a publisher publish it anyway. To be honest, I tried to read it and got bogged down early on.

Fast forward to today. After TJI (The Jenkins Institute) began its publishing wing, Tracy mentioned the book to me again. Now, I had no excuse - I had the tools to bring it to print. I picked it up, and within a couple of pages I was hooked by the concept.

This is a book that every congregation I know about needs to study. I think it would keep peace in the church and decrease misunderstandings that lead to hard feelings. I think it could negate conflict that makes it simple for people to slip out "the back door." While I may not have seen it a few years back, I think Tracy is really onto something. Most people don't want to be in conflict.

If you are an elder, deacon, minister, or teacher—frankly, if you are involved at all in your congregation, you know that challenges arise. We know they are often personality driven and beg for satisfactory resolution.

If we could learn to understand and appreciate each other's differences, to see the other's personality at work instead of questioning motives and character, wouldn't it improve the health of the church? If we begin to see how their strengths aid the work of the Lord and gain insight on how to work with them, surely that would be healthy in a local setting.

I want to encourage you to read this book and then perhaps to use it as a study guide for adult classes or groups in your congregation. I think you'll see "fruit" from it. Thank you Tracy, for being a good friend, and for not giving up on seeing that this study has a wider influence.

Dale Jenkins ~ TheJenkinsInstitute.com

INTRODUCTION

It was the monthly social for our senior citizens. A couple of men and I were talking about things that had happened in the church in times past and how people reacted to them, some good and some not so good. After a lengthy discussion one of the men said, "Some people are like that." Have you ever made statements like this? Have you ever noticed that some people deal with things differently than you or others do? Many times it is personality that causes that difference.

Hippocrates, the Greek physician and philosopher, believed that people acted a certain way because of their body liquid. He thought the four temperament types were the result of four kinds of body liquids within the human body. He gave names to these personalities that suggested the liquid type; the Sanguine – blood, Choleric – yellow bile, Melancholy – black bile, and Phlegmatic – phlegm. They represented lively, active, black, and slow temperaments.

I was assigned a class on these four personalities while working on my Master's degree. The class was based upon the work of Florence Littauer and her materials entitled *Your Personality Tree*. Her work was also based on the temperament studies of Hippocrates. It was fascinating, and the study helped me to put together the missing pieces to the puzzle of personalities in society, more especially the church. Her work answered some important questions such as:

- Why do people act a certain way?
- Why do I get along with some people but not with others?
- How do I get along with those difficult people in my life?

Since that time studying temperaments has become a hobby of mine. I have purchased every book Florence Littauer has published and any others I can find based on this model. The more I read, the more I realize the need for such a book in the church. Think about it for a minute, what is the church? We have said for years it is not a building. The Bible tells us it is the people (1 Cor. 12:27). Most of our problems come from personality related issues and not doctrinal errors. Almost everything that happens with our congregations is the direct result of temperaments. This is why I believe this study is so important.

First of all, it will help us understand ourselves. How we express ourselves outwardly is the direct result of our inner personality. How many times have we heard young people go on these long journeys to "find themselves" or to find out who they are inside? Sometimes it is a matter of learning more of their personality. No doubt difficult life events can cloud that understanding, but this study can go a long way. It will help you know your strengths and to grow in them. It will also help you to see your weaknesses and help you to eliminate them.

Additionally a study of the personalities will help us understand others. The Hebrew writer urges us to "consider how to stir up one another to love and good works" (Heb. 10:24, ESV). Why do some Christians seem so optimistic and others seem so negative? Why do some people do everything they can to be out front and others do everything they can to stay behind the scenes? How can some folks always tell you what's on their mind while others are not willing to tell you the most basic information? Who are these people and why do they act a certain way? These are just some of the questions we will attempt to answer.

Anytime you work with a group of people with varying personalities there will be problems, even for Christians. Just because we are supposed to act like Christians doesn't mean there will not be human relation issues. Most church splits are the direct result of personality conflicts - not theological issues. This includes the style of preaching we prefer, the songs we enjoy in worship, and the color of paint on the walls. It is the Lord who adds us to the church (Acts 2:47), and when He does we are mixed in with all types of varying personalities. To have true unity we must be willing to understand one another, and personalities. Having the basics of Christianity is not enough, and we will prove that fact by noticing several Biblical examples.

In Philippians 4:1-3, Paul addresses the church at Philippi about a conflict between two sisters in Christ – Euodia and Syntyche. The division would not have been over doctrinal issues but relational problems or personality issues. Paul doesn't go into detail about the dispute, but since he doesn't take sides, it indicates it was a personal matter. He only mentions that both of them were committed Christians who worked hard for the Lord's church. This is why it is important to learn about people.

The purpose of this book is not to be a complete work of why people react and behave as they do. There are many aspects to human behavior including gender, birth order, family history, physical and mental challenges. I do believe this will help in understanding the people you encounter every day.

Something else: No one person is 100% of any of these personalities, although some may come close at times. Usually everyone has a dominant and a secondary personality type. Some may have a dominant and two secondary types. One of those may dominate at your work place and another your home life. There are many aspects to understanding the personalities but it is not as difficult as this may sound.

Finally, understand that this book is not a cure all. Some have greater needs than learning about their temperament. For example, just because one is impatient does not mean they are choleric or sanguine. It could be a physical or psychological problem. Several years ago I baptized a lady who was searching for something missing in her life. I taught her about Jesus Christ, and she came forward the following Sunday wanting to be baptized. She seemed so happy and fulfilled that day. That night she came back and told me she was so thrilled about what happened that morning that she walked across the street to be baptized at the Methodist Church. I was surprised to say the least. A few days passed, and I started learning more about her and found out she was bi-polar with multiple personality disorder and exhibited twenty-one personalities! It wasn't long after this she called me at 3:00 in the morning to tell me Jesus had come back to earth and was now living in her. As you may already know, this book is not going to do her much good, God bless her. My prayer is that it will help many individuals and most especially the church overall.

Here is an overall review of the personalities. Be sure to read the next page - it will help you understand these unusual terms.

Extroverts	S Sanguine	C Choleric
Introverts	P Phlegmatic	M Melancholy

Before we go any further
THIS WILL HELP YOU UNDERSTAND THIS BOOK

Those who have read and reviewed this book have been so very gracious in their help but almost all of them have said basically the same thing: "These titles are not ones that I am familiar with and I find myself getting lost in them." And they are correct. Most who read use this material are not professional counselors and/or in the field of sociology so we are going to give you a few easier to remember terms that we'll reference often to "bring you back on page" and help you focus. These are not perfect descriptors but should be a help in making the material more digestible:

The sanguine (aka Life of the party)
The choleric (aka The Leader)
The melancholy (aka The Perfectionist)
The phlegmatic (aka The Peacemaker)

For those visual learners it might help you to think of cars with the personalities. I have used this often in seminars.

Sanguines are flashy and ready for adventure.
Cholerics can plow through anything to complete a goal.
Melancholies are the geniuses of society and very economical.
Phlegmatics always strive for peace.

Extroverts		
	Sanguine (The Life of the Party)	Choleric (The Leader)
Introverts		
	Phlegmatic (The Peacemaker)	Melancholy (The Perfectionist)

CHAPTER 1

MEET THE CONGREGATION

Sam and Samantha Sanguine - The Life of the Party

While attending Faulkner University in Montgomery, Alabama, I was fortunate to take a class entitled *The Preacher and His Work*. It was based on the book written by Jack Meyer, Sr., along with the life experiences and studies of our instructor Wendell Winkler. It was one of the most helpful classes I took as a young minister.

One of the lessons, a section called "Meet the Congregation," opened up a door to many unforgettable characters that we find in every congregation: such people as, "Mr. Come-on Strong," and "Mr. Waste Your Time," and of course "Mr. Chip on his Shoulder," etc. This was my first taste into the world of personalities in the church.

The first four chapters, of this book, are an introduction of the different temperament types. Every one of us have them in our churches and now it is time for you to *meet the congregation*.

Our first couple is Sam and Samantha Sanguine. They are a fun loving couple with the most appealing personality. Hippocrates thought they had fiery red blood shooting through their veins. Let me give you some ways of identifying this couple. We'll refer to them also as " The life of the party" - because THEY ARE.

SANGUINE POSITIVES

LIFE-GIVERS

You know them as soon as they enter the front doors of the church building. They are always filled with energy and life. They can literally light up the room when they come into Bible class. It is a natural charisma that draws others to them. These are the people wearing smiles and saying positive things. In fact, sanguines are enthusiastic over almost everything. They love the new songs; they like it when the elders present new works; they get excited about new Bible classes. Whatever you bring up, they want to do it. We need this in the church. The apostle Paul wrote, *"Whatever you do, work heartily…"* (Col. 3:23) In other words, with enthusiasm!

Peter is the prime example of this type of personality. Just like most sanguines, he was always moving, talking, and demonstrating energy. Peter *fell down at Jesus' knees* (Lk. 5:8); *ran* to the tomb of Christ (Lk. 24:12); *threw himself into the sea* when he heard that it was the Lord on the shore (Jn. 21:7). He was a great orator who knew how to capture the attention of a crowd. He *stood up among the…hundred and twenty* (Acts 1:15). Peter *directed his gaze at him…and said, "Look at us"* (Acts 3:4). Peter was constantly using his hands. Notice Acts 12:17 where he motioned for the disciples to quiet down so he could speak (typical sanguine to get everyone quiet while he speaks).

Peter was the spokesman for the group, constantly speaking out (Matt. 14:28, 15:15, 16:16, 17:4, 18:21, 19:27; Mk. 11:21; Lk. 8:45; 12:41; Jn. 6:68, 13:6, 13:37, 21:21; Acts 2:15, 38, 3:4, 12, 4:8, 13, 5:3, 8:20, 9:34, 10:34). He was the one that the people related to the most (Matt. 17:24; Jn. 20:2; Acts 5:15, 9:38, 10:2). Peter had a commanding presence.

The sanguine loves church get-togethers. They are a great example of Christian hospitality (1Pe. 4:9). Not only that, but they usually organize the best functions. If you show up at their house during Christmas you will see the glow of the lights before you see the neighborhood. When you walk in be prepared to see more lights, multiple Christmas trees, bright colors of red and green, along with the sounds of Christmas blaring throughout the house. Don't be surprised if they have on the newest Christmas sweater in their collection and are eating one of their famous Santa Claus shaped sandwiches, while drinking punch from a reindeer mug. It is a sanguine party.

These are not the kind of people who need to live in a subdivision with rules and regulations. Those places try to keep everything uniform with matching mailboxes, privacy fences, and manicured yards. The sanguines like individuality and feel it is their job to add color to what seems to be dull. For whatever reason, some people do not like bases painted in the cul-de-sac so kids can play games. Some do not understand the beauty of a big mouth bass as a mailbox or the fun of flying a pirates flag in the front lawn. The kids on the street love them and some neighbors enjoy the entertainment, but not everyone does.

MOTIVATORS

A sanguine has natural charisma that inspires others to follow them. Their energy and excitement is contagious. They can charm almost anyone into carrying out their ideas.

Remember the story of *Tom Sawyer*? One of my favorite parts is the time Tom was told to paint the fence around the yard. Terrible job, but he somehow convinced the neighborhood children that painting the fence was fun. Next thing you know kids were begging him to let them participate and were willing to give up their own possessions for the honor. That is the real ability of a sanguine.

God knew it would take a great motivator to lead His church into world. The day the church began, Peter was chosen to preach that first gospel message. He was to motivate his countrymen and women to become a part of the new covenant of Christ. Remember, many of these people had yelled for the Lord to be crucified a little over a month before, and by the way, the day this lesson was to be delivered was during the Jewish festival of Pentecost – Old Law. He had a few hecklers at the outset (Acts 2:15), but with the help of the Holy Spirit he motivated about 3,000 to commit to Christ (Acts 2:41). By the time he got finished speaking Peter was able to move from the surface to the heart of the people (Acts 2:37).

Things sailed along for a few years and Christ was ready to open up the doors to the Gentiles. These were the enemies of the Jews and it was not going to be easy. Peter is the one chosen to deal with the issue. He was not the apostle chosen to take the message to them, as this would fall upon Paul, but to lead the way. First God had to convince him (Acts 10:9-16) and then He sent a Gentile to Peter to be given the Good News of Christ. The Holy Spirit came upon them to show that God had accepted them as He had Jewish Christians (Acts 10:44-48). Peter is the one who is chosen to convince the others that this is what God wants.

To see the influence Peter had on the church all you have to do is look to 1 Corinthians 1 and see those who had become sole followers of his. It wasn't what Peter wanted, but it demonstrates his influence. In Galatians 2:11-21 Peter stopped eating with the Gentiles and the rest of the Jews followed suit. Again, not the plans of God, but people followed Peter. This is the guy who helped keep the Christians from getting discouraged during times of persecution and avoid following false prophets (1 and 2 Peter).

A sanguine is a master motivator and can accomplish great things.

PEOPLE-PLEASER

The sanguine can be self-centered but they do like to please others. This goes along with their desire to be popular. They like for others to feel comfortable around them. They want people to like them.

This is not a bad quality in the church. Too many times we are more concerned about ourselves than we are the feelings of those around us. The sanguines get their greatest satisfaction from pleasing others and love the applause of the audience.

Jesus asked the disciples, *Who do people say that the Son of Man is?* (Matt. 16:13) Many answers were given and the Lord wanted to hear what they thought. Peter speaks up, *You are the Christ, the Son of the living God.* (Matt. 16:16) Jesus was very pleased with this answer and gave Peter the proverbial keys to the kingdom of heaven.

Later Peter seems to try and please Jesus with his question, "Lord, how often will my brother sin against me and I forgive him? As many as seven times?" (Matt. 18:21). The rabbis taught you only had to forgive others three times since God only forgave Israel's enemies three times (Amos 1:3,6,9,11,13). Peter is putting it on heavy to please God. Not necessarily a bad thing, but it illustrated his desire to please. He eventually reminded the Lord of the sacrifices the apostles had made to follow him (Matt. 19:27).

A sanguine is a great person. I have served congregations that had elderly people who gave candy to the kids. Of course they were a favorite and the children always sought them out as they entered the building. Yet, it was the one giving the candy that was getting the most out of it as those smiling faces would approach them and hugs were exchanged.

Being an impulsive personality, you often find sanguines doing things for others on the spur of the moment. One Sunday I witnessed a member commenting to a true sanguine about his tie. He took it off and gave it to the guy. They really understand the idea that "it is more blessed to give than to receive." (Acts 20:35.) This personality is uplifting to the church (Rom. 15:1-3).

SANGUINE NEGATIVES

One of the great statements of Florence Littauer was something like, "strengths carried to extremes become weaknesses" or "you go in on your strengths and you leave on your weaknesses." In other words, while every temperament has definite positives, if they are not under control, they can turn into negatives.

COMPULSIVE TALKER

A sanguine loves to talk. This can be a real positive, but taken to extremes it becomes a negative. It becomes the opposite of James' admonition to be "*quick to hear, slow to speak*" (Jms. 1:19), and twists it to *slow to hear and quick to speak.*

Can you think of a better example than Peter? He was a little quick to blurt out in the middle of a storm "*Lord, if it is you, command me to come to you on the water*" (Matt. 14:28). Let us not forget that Peter had never seen anyone do this before. And it was in the middle of a raging storm. It would come back to bite him (v. 30). In Matthew 16:21-23 we find Peter trying to correct Christ about His announcement that He would die. He meant well, but he spoke before he thought it through. On the Mount of Transfiguration (Matt. 17:1-13) rather than listening he blurted out that he would like to build three shrines. Peter missed the whole point of that great event because he was too busy talking and not doing enough listening. In John 13:3-9, Jesus bends down to wash Peter's feet as the Lord was trying to teach them an important lesson. Peter blurts out, *You shall never wash my feet.* Jesus tried to help him understand the importance of what he was doing but Peter blurts out "*Lord, not my feet only but also my hands and my head!*" Peter just listen. Then there was the whole Last Supper scene where Jesus predicted someone would deny Him three times (Matt. 26:31-35). Peter immediately speaks (without thinking) "*Even if I must die with you, I will never deny you!*" There would be some crow to eat soon.

A sanguine doesn't like silence or dead spaces. They feel compelled to keep a conversation going so they naturally talk to keep things from getting boring. What they don't realize is compulsive talking is boring to those listening. It was Solomon who wrote, *a word in season, how good it is!* (Prov. 15:23). In other words, use your words wisely and not merely as a filler for dead conversation. This well-meaning personality can dominate a Bible class discussion, interrupt others while they are talking, and have a comment on everything the church is doing.

When our tongue is working harder than our ears the "foot in mouth" principle comes into play. As a sanguine, I have put my foot in my mouth so many times I have almost acquired a taste for it. It isn't that sanguines want to hurt other people but they do not think before they speak. When I was a young minister, I visited a member in the hospital who had just had his leg amputated. As with similar circumstances it is difficult to know what to say, but being a sanguine I felt it was my duty to say something (big mistake). No sooner had this man told me he would be going home the next day; I blurted out, "I bet you hit the door *running*, when they told you." At that moment, this personality's greatest fear happened – silence and a loss for words. He had told me a couple of weeks before how much he hated hospitals, and that is what prompted my remark. I meant well but should have thought before I spoke. I felt awful.

Proverbs 10:19 says "*When words are many, transgression is not lacking, but whoever restrains his lips is prudent.*"

EXAGGERATOR

One of the unique qualities of a sanguine is telling stories. They put so much energy and enthusiasm into telling stories and they are entertaining. However, they are prone to over exaggerate parts of the story. They can take a small event and turn it into something worthy of a book and movie deal.

This can be due to their underlying need to be accepted. Some think the better the story the more they are liked. What is amazing is their story can grow every time they tell it to someone else. I directed a week of camp while preaching at a congregation in Alabama. We would carry a large group of young people and adults every summer. One year we had two eight-year-old boys who came for the first time. They were very entertaining kids who were often into mischief, but very popular on campus (typical sanguine). During the week they saw a snake in the woods. It was about three feet long and a couple of inches thick, but that snake grew every time they told someone about their encounter. By the following Sunday the snake had grown ten feet and developed a mouth full of fangs. A sanguine child can really get into a story.

This is cute in children, but when those children turn into adults the stories become trouble. Sanguines can lose the trust of others, because people will not know if what you are telling is truth or fiction. Also, over exaggeration can be annoying.

Peter could exaggerate the moment, as illustrated at the Last Supper. Once Jesus told him he could not be a part of Him if he didn't wash his feet, he suddenly turned and said *"Lord, do not wash my feet only but also my hands and my head!"* (Jn. 13:9). That was a pretty quick jump.

OVER IMPULSIVE

Because sanguines love fun they will often do things on the spur of the moment. There was a Christian family in Nashville that decided to take a Sunday drive one afternoon. They kept driving until they ended up in Florida! They had to buy some clothes, bathroom supplies, and food once they got there. That is pretty extreme, even for a sanguine, and yes, the father of that family was a total sanguine.

Being impulsive is not a bad thing, but sometimes you have to be careful. This personality has good intentions and often does things that feel right. Yet, the Bible warns us about letting our emotions rule our actions (Prov. 19:2; Rom. 10:2).

We are right back to Peter and the time of Jesus' betrayal and arrest in the garden. Peter draws his sword and cuts off Malchus' ear (Jn. 18:3-11). He had good intentions, but it wasn't God's plan. A sanguine doesn't always go through the proper channels to figure out what should be done. They do not mean to over-step their bounds.

I know of a congregation that did some renovations to their building. The elders hired an interior decorator to come in and set up a plan so the building would have a continuous flow throughout. A well-meaning sanguine member decided to do their part and made some homemade items for one of the newly decorated rooms. They did a good job, the only problem was it clashed with the colors of the room. They meant well, but it would have been much better had they checked with the decorator on the colors and style for the new room.

Sam and Samantha Sanguine are a colorful couple within the church. They bring a life that is so desperately needed in every congregation.

CHAPTER 2

MEET THE CONGREGATION

Chris and Christy Choleric - The Leader

Chris and Christy Choleric are the second couple you find sitting in the pews. Like Sam and Samantha Sanguine, they are extroverts with outgoing personalities. Yet, they are uniquely different in many ways. A Hummer well represents this couple who can plow through anything to complete a goal. Remember the Cholerics as the Leaders.

CHOLERIC POSITIVES

SUCCESSFUL

Cholerics have the ability to succeed at almost anything they put their minds to. They can achieve and move up the ladder of success despite obstacles they may face along the way.

My mother is a classic example of a choleric leader. She decided to try and make extra money by signing up to sell cosmetics. In the first year she became the second highest sales representative in her district, about 10,000 people, and the #1 sales representative in the state of Alabama. Within three years, she became a director within the corporation, drove their famous pink Cadillac, and earned trips to Europe and Canada. She won many awards, jewelry, a fur coat, and other prizes for her achievements. By the way, my mother had never worn make-up until this time, unless it was a special occasion (funeral, wedding, etc.). She also lived in the small town of Hamilton, Alabama (population 5,000). She had a drive to succeed and a natural power of persuasion.

Within the church, these are the Christians who have successfully helped to launch the church into the world. They are your members who go door to door in hot summer weather to invite people to services. These are the people who helped think up, coordinate, and operate the many successful ministries of the church. They are the founders of our Christian Universities, camps, and other great programs for the church worldwide. These are the ones who helped plant churches all over the globe.

The apostle Paul is the classic choleric personality. Here was a man who was very successful in life, before and after his conversion. He had been trained as a Pharisee and tentmaker. In Acts 8:1-3 we learn he was a powerful man, getting permission to travel to Damascus to capture Christians and bring them back to Jerusalem. Yet, his greatest work would come after he became a disciple of Christ. He helped to plant and strengthen the Lord's church throughout the Roman Empire on three missionary journeys (Acts 13-21). Paul penned the majority of the New Testament, and became one of the most vital members of the New Testament church. He is an example of a choleric dedicated to Christianity.

LEADER

The choleric has a charisma that people naturally follow. Many people claim to be leaders and some are even forced into leadership positions, but only those who can get others to follow them are true leaders. Like the saying, "He who thinketh he leadeth and hath no one following him is only taking a walk."

My mother was not only successful selling cosmetics, but she also helped many other ladies accomplish great things in the company. As a director, she helped her group to make more money than any other group in the state. She would help four other women, among her own circle, to become successful directors as well. That is the fruit of leadership.

The apostle Paul demonstrated the potential of a choleric who submits to God completely. He had a tremendous influence on the churches throughout the Roman Empire. He was a true leader. After his conversion he had an immediate influence on the church (Acts 9:20-22). We are given a glimpse of his leadership capability while handling the explosive situation within the Corinthian church. These young Christians were struggling to live godly lives in the immoral society of Corinth. The church had become divided (1 Cor. 1:10-17). They faced such issues as sexual immorality (5:1-2; 6:9-11), suing each other (6:1), marriage problems (7:1ff) and idolatry (10:1ff). They were struggling over matters of worship, even the Lord's Supper (11:17-34), and spiritual gifts (1 Cor. 12:1ff). Although many of them were hostile towards Paul, he wrote a letter to those Christians that would resolve the matter. Only a man of great influence could resolve church problems with a letter. He would use this means several times while imprisoned in Rome. Paul commissioned Titus to complete the work of the church on the island of Crete by appointing elders in every city (Titus 1:5). Titus helped to guide congregations in appointing elders in various congregations (Acts 14:23). Spiritual leaders have the ability to influence others. I doubt there is any eldership that does not have at least one choleric personality. When guided by God and His Word, cholerics can do great things for the cause of Christ.

PERSISTENT

My grandfather was a good example of this temperament. He was raised in a poor family as one of five boys. Later on in life, he decided to attend Freed-Hardeman

University in hopes of becoming a preacher. As a dominant Choleric, he was determined to get an education, even though he did not have any money. He jumped train cars and hitched hiked from his home to college. Brother N.B. Hardeman allowed him to go to school on scholarship for a semester free (actually he had to milk the cows every morning). However, he was called into brother Hardeman's office the second semester and asked if he had the money to pay for another term. My grandfather said he didn't and Brother Hardeman told him he was withdrawing his scholarship because he "didn't have what it takes to preach." Other personalities would have given up, but not the persistent choleric. My grandfather left Brother Hardeman's office and hitched hiked to Memphis, Tennessee to find a job. He walked into a garment factory and inquired about a position. He got the job, and due to his poor lifestyle growing up, he was able to live on a small amount of money and save the rest. Eventually he saved enough money to start his own garment company along with two other partners in Hamilton, Alabama. In time, he bought out the other two men and built a thriving business making shirts. He was an American success story. You can find many such stories among the choleric temperament.

We go back to our choleric example, the apostle Paul. He didn't let obstacles keep him from succeeding. After his conversion (Acts 9), the Jewish leaders (those he had been working for) set out to kill him (Acts 9:23-25). Add to that, his new brothers and sisters in Christ did not trust him (Acts 9:26). Later on he had to deal with some physical problems (2 Cor. 12:7-8). These things would slow him down but never stopped him from succeeding in the kingdom of God. This doesn't even take into account the number of times he faced death. Five times the Jews gave him thirty-nine lashes with a whip, three times he was beaten with rods, once he was stoned (and left for dead – Acts 14:19-20), and four times shipwrecked. Nor does this include the constant dangers in his travels, such as flooded rivers, stormy seas, deserts, robbers, and even the problems he faced with his own people. He lived with fatigue, pain, sleepless nights, hunger, thirst, and the cold (2 Cor. 11:24-27). Through it all Paul never gave up. He never threw up his hands and said "I've had enough." Other personalities are more prone to give in when the going gets tough, but the choleric can feed off of hard times. The most motivating thing you can tell a choleric is they cannot do something.

Paul wrote, in 2 Corinthians 4:16, "So we do not lose heart…" Another translation says, "We never give up" (NLT).

CHOLERIC NEGATIVES

PRIDE

Because a choleric is successful they can be tempted to pride. It is easy for anyone with great accomplishments to believe all their ability comes from within and not give credit or glory to God. This pride ultimately leads to failure as Proverbs 16:18 teaches,

Pride goes before destruction,
and a haughty spirit before a fall.

King Saul is a great example of a choleric gone bad. He had everything a leader needs – looks, courage, and determination, but his pride prevented him from reaching his ultimate goals. At first he gave God the credit for victories (1 Sam. 11:13), but it wasn't long before he started to believe he was the reason for the successes and there were many such victories over the Moabites, Ammonites, Edomites, the kings of Zobah, the Philistines and the Amalekites (1 Sam. 14:47-48). It all went to his head. On one particular occasion the prophet Samuel sought out Saul after a great victory, because he had not been completely obedient (1 Sam. 15:10). When Samuel arrived he learned that Saul had gone to Carmel to set up a monument to himself (15:12). This was the beginning of the end for King Saul (15:10-23). Saul teaches us that our personality strengths should be used as tools in the hands of an All-powerful God, but when we no longer recognize the Lord in our achievements, we will not be able to reach our full potential.

The same can happen in the church. Yes, the church, where God allows us to succeed. Ministers, elders, and individual members can believe their sermons and plans, not God, brought the increase. A dangerous road to failure (1 Cor. 3:6).

Even King David struggled with this aspect as a choleric leader. On one occasion he took a census of Israel and Judah (2 Sam. 24), which was basically a military draft. Seems harmless but it was motivated out of pride and ambition. The nation was at peace so their was no need to enlist troops – David wanted to know the size and glory of his army. This indicated that he had put his faith in the size of his army rather than God's ability to care for them.

Church leaders must be careful not to let their success become their downfall.

CONTROLLING

A choleric likes to be in control and we do well to put them in charge. A positive trait, but when taken to extremes it becomes a negative.

My family is littered with controlling choleric temperaments. I can remember taking trips to Disney World as a kid with my grandparents, aunts and uncles, cousins, and of course, my parents and siblings. We exceeded our quota of controlling personalities. It was especially apparent with my mother and aunt. They had a plan to conquer the parks in a matter of days. We had to be ready at a certain time so we could arrive several minutes before the gates were opened. Once they were unlocked we were to advance "swiftly" to the reservation center to make dinner plans for the night. Then we were to move "promptly" to a certain section of the park until everything was ridden, explored and conquered. Then we were off to the next section where we continued the routine. If you could not keep up you were to go back to the hotel and meet back at the appointed time and location. Only a choleric can take the fun out of the "Happiest place on earth." By the end of the trip we were ready to stuff both of them in Cinderella's castle and go home without them. They were over-controlling. Leadership is good, but carried to extremes becomes a negative.

Paul seemed to be controlling at times. There was "a sharp disagreement" between Paul and Barnabas (Acts 15:39). Even though Barnabas wanted to carry John Mark on this missionary campaign Paul was not going to allow it to happen because John Mark had left them on the last trip. Barnabas, the man who was known to be an encourager, parted ways with Paul. This did not stop Paul, who picked up Silas to continue this mission.

Yet, a better example of a choleric gone bad would have to be Diotrephes. 3 John 9-10 says, "*I have written something to the church, but Diotrephes, who likes to put himself first, does not acknowledge our authority… he refuses to welcome the brothers, and also stops those who want to and puts them out of the church.*" Here is a man who loved to be in control of the church. The text indicates he wanted others to serve him. This is the very opposite of what Jesus taught His disciples (Jn. 13:12-17; 20:20-28).

Choleric Paul taught, by the inspiration of the Spirit, that an elder (leader) in the church is not to be *arrogant* (Titus 1:7), which means one who is "dominated by self-interest, and inconsiderate of others." Peter said true elders are *not domineering over those in their charge, but lead by being examples to the flock.* (1 Pet. 5:3)

Wise churches will avoid selecting domineering leaders. There can be members sitting in your pew who want to take charge of the church. They can cause serious problems, tearing down godly leadership, and always challenging every decision made, while recruiting others to follow them.

DISCONTENT

The choleric can be very discontent because of their nature to achieve. They are always looking for ways to make more money, climb up higher ladders, and build bigger companies. These are your workaholics. They enjoy the long hours because it gives them more opportunities to conquer the next obstacles.

The nature of a choleric leads them to reject mediocrity. Carried to extremes this attitude turns into dissatisfaction. We need the choleric nature to make sure the church doesn't become lax and content with past growth. However, the problem arises when they become discontent with the growth the Lord provided. In other words, they feel as if the church has failed if it didn't reach their desired goals of baptisms and yearly growth. The fact is, sometimes the church decreases or remains the same because of a string of deaths, people moving away, or other events. The choleric must never forget the words of 1 Corinthians 3:6, "*I planted, Apollos watered, but God gave the growth.*" The church does not grow because I put in so many hours a week; it grows because the Lord blesses the work. We are to do our part, but only God receives credit for the increase.

Contentment is a natural trait of a phlegmatic, but not so with a choleric. The apostle Paul, our dominant choleric, said he "*learned in whatever situation* to be content" (Phil. 4:11 emp. TM). It did not come naturally for him. God gave him some teaching moments with the thorn in the flesh. In 2 Corinthians 12:8-10 Paul writes "*Three times I pleaded with the Lord about this, that it should leave me. But he said to me, 'My grace is sufficient for you, for my power is made perfect in weakness.' Therefore I will boast all the more gladly of my weaknesses, so that the power of Christ may rest upon me. For the sake of Christ, then, I am content with weaknesses, insults, hardships, persecutions, and calamities. For when I am weak, then I am strong.*"

When cholerics learn the art of contentment, they will be better family members, business associates, preachers, elders, and goal-oriented believers. Chris and Christy Choleric will be able to influence the church in powerful ways.

CHAPTER 3

MEET THE CONGREGATION

Melvin and Melissa Melancholy-The Perfectionist

Unlike the first two couples we met, Melvin and Melissa Melancholy are introverts. Of course, there are many other qualities that make them different than just having a quiet nature. In fact, how they view a study of the personalities is somewhat different. The sanguine enjoys a study like this because it is fun. The choleric sees the value of learning about the nature of people to help them be more effective leaders. The phlegmatic is just content to study what everyone else wants, but to the melancholy they are not so sure they can be put into a box. They see themselves as complex and this personality testing isn't as detailed as some of the others offered. Once they understand the temperaments they will enjoy this study much more than the other personalities. We'll remember the Melancholys as The Perfectionists. Each time you read "melancholy" think "Smart Car" - not wasting anything and learning from everything.

MELANCHOLY POSITIVES

ANALYTICAL

The melancholy is the thinker of the group. They analyze things before they move one way or another. They know what they want to do and how to get there. The melancholy is the genius of society. These are the people who graduate Valedictorians of their class, answer the million dollar question on game shows, and figure out the puzzles of life. Without them our world would be less advanced in medicine, literature, architecture, education or even theology. Their search for truth is more important to them than being famous or favored by their peers. Solomon, said,

The beginning of wisdom is this: Get wisdom,
And whatever you get, get insight.

Speaking of Solomon, he is a great example of a melancholy temperament. God appeared to him, after becoming the new king, in a dream and basically said, "your wish is my command." (1 Kings. 3:5) Solomon answered like the typical melancholy, he said, *"Give your servant therefore an understanding mind to govern your people, that I may discern between good and evil…"* (1 Kings. 3:9). Only a melancholy would ask for wisdom. The sanguine would have wanted an extended vacation on a cruise to some of the more exciting places around the Holy Lands. The choleric would have asked for riches and power, yet, the melancholy understands that knowledge is power. God replied *"Because you have asked this, and have not asked for yourself long life or riches or the life of your enemies, but have asked for yourself understanding to discern what is right, behold, I now do according to your word. Behold, I give you a wisdom and discerning mind… I will give you also what you have not asked, both riches and honor…"* (1 Kings. 3:11-13).

We need this type of personality in the church. In fact, when the Bible speaks about *wisdom* it is talking about the wisdom of God and not the wisdom of man. We live in a society that believes everything and anything is all right as long as you love God. We need Christians who are committed to truth, rather than subjective experiences (Prov. 14:12), human reasoning (Jer. 10:23), the practice of the majority (Matt. 7:13,14), our conscience (Acts 23:1), our feelings (Gen. 37:23), or human traditions (2 Thess. 3:6). The church needs analytical minds where truth is more important than popularity or politics.

ORGANIZED

My wife is a dominant Melancholy. She is one of the most organized people I know. When our boys were younger she had the playroom structured so action figures would go in one box, blocks in another, cars in their designated places, etc. her favorite magazine is a catalogue that sells household organizers. My attic and garage is filled with those big buckets you get at Wal-Mart. Melissa fills them with clothes, shoes, toys, decorations, and miscellaneous items. But what made it even better is the fact they are color coordinated. Green is hers, blue are the children's, maroon is mine, and clear represented gift wrapping materials (one for bags, another for wrapping paper, another for bows, and one more for strings). Each box is labeled with a description of everything inside (sizes, styles, usage, etc.). When we married I became her worst nightmare. Being dominant sanguine, I had a tendency to be disorganized. I lived out of a laundry basket, doesn't everyone? Why use drawers when you can have everything in one basket? Everything I needed was in that basket and if we had company I would simply throw my basket in the closet. It was a good system for me, but it drove my melancholy wife crazy. After several years of marriage I now use drawers and shelves. A melancholy must have organization.

We serve an organized God. When man sinned in the garden, God had an organized way to bring mankind back to Him (Gen. 3:15; 1 Pet. 1:20). He methodically chose the seed of Abraham to establish His nation (Gen. 12:1-3), and would organize them in the wilderness to set up His laws (Ex. 19-22), regulations (Ex. 23:20-33), and a structured place of worship, the tabernacle (Ex. 25-27), along with a priesthood (Ex. 28-29). It would be through this nation the Messiah would come into the world (Matt. 1). Christ would establish a new form of organization while on earth – His church (Matt. 16:18). Just like the old law, the law of Christ would be well organized. John the Baptizer was sent before hand to prepare the Lord's ministry (Mk. 1:1-8), and twelve men were chosen to carry out His ministry (Lk. 6:12-16). Even the death and resurrection of the Son of God was in the plan (Matt. 27:26-50; 28:1-8). When the church age began God gave it structure through doctrine (Gal. 1:6-9), worship (I Cor. 11:2-34), and leadership (I Tim. 3:1-7). The apostle Paul spoke of God's organization when he said, *God has appointed in the church first apostles, second prophets, third teachers, then miracles, then gifts of healing, helping, administrating, and various kinds of tongues* (1 Cor. 12:28). The melancholy, like the other personalities, is a piece of God's nature.

We need that organized nature within the church. When the Corinthian worship became chaotic, Paul wrote *"But all things should be done decently and in order"* (1 Cor. 14:40). Without the melancholy we would probably have chaos and confusion, the opposite of God (1 Cor. 14:33). Can you imagine having a building program without a melancholy? The sanguine could get everyone excited about it and the choleric could raise the funds and manpower to build it, but the melancholy provides a safe, economical, and sound plan.

I refer back to our melancholy King Solomon. Have you ever noticed his well thought-out plans in the building of the temple? He enlisted 30,000 workers from all over Israel. These men worked in shifts (10,000 men every month), and would work one month at a time and have two months at home. They enlisted 70,000 common workers, 80,000 stonecutters, and 3,600 foremen to supervise these non-Israelite working crews (1 Kings. 6:1-37; 7:13-51). This intricate plan took them seven years to build. When his palace went up the same detailed planning was put in place.

TALENTED

Florence Littauer, in her book *Personality Plus*, wrote, "Without Perfect Melancholy's we would have little poetry, art, literature, philosophy, or symphonies. We would be missing the culture, refinement, taste, and talent so deep within our natures. We would have fewer engineers, inventors, scientist; or ledgers might be lost and our columns wouldn't balance." In other words, they are the most gifted of all the personalities.

Stan Ball was a deacon with a congregation I served in Nashville. He was a jack of all trades. Stan is a surgical assistant in great demand, who invented surgical tools and served as the Director of Surgical Services before deciding to take on carpentry. His work is a work of art as he turns old homes, garages, and patios into beautiful modern places. He uses many original ideas making his work unique. Stan also paints professional pictures, winning several awards from the Central South Art Exhibits. He was invited to join the Tennessee Art League (a prestigious organization for artists) and creates beautiful outdoor fountains. As you can imagine, Stan has been a great blessing to this church. One year, for Vacation Bible School, he constructed a running stream in one of the classrooms to create the perfect setting for David and Goliath. He painted and built a Victorian house for puppets for the children's classes. He paid attention to the details as he painted trees, animals, etc. on the walls, along with several other murals in the classrooms.

King David, while he had some choleric qualities, also had many melancholy traits. He was one of the most talented men in the Bible. We know he had been a talented young musician (1 Sam. 16:16-18). He was a songwriter and poet of many Psalms. David was also a great general in the Lord's army (2 Sam. 8), even taking a group of outcasts and turning them into powerful fighting machines (1 Sam. 22:1-2). He was handy with a slingshot (1 Sam. 17:49).

If there is ever a five talent Christian, the melancholy would fit that description.

MELANCHOLY NEGATIVES

DEPRESSED

Every personality gets depressed for a variety of reasons but the melancholy is the most susceptible. In fact, one of the definitions of this word means, "sad, gloomy, or depressed." The ancients used the words *melancholy* and *depression* interchangeably. They seem to get disappointed easier than the other temperaments and have a harder time getting over that gloominess. This is due to their unrealistic view of the world. The melancholy is a perfectionist who likes organization – our world is neither. Since man sinned in the Garden of Eden the world has been ruled by imperfection and chaos. Even the punishment of man and woman would assure this to be the case. Woman was doomed to a life of pain and suffering through childbirth. She was commanded to be in submission to her man (Gen. 3:16). God's sentence to the man was that he would be sentenced to a life of strenuous labor. Their sin affected all of God's creation. Sin is the source of an imperfect world. Even perfectionists sin (1 Jn. 1:8-10). Until a melancholy understands this point, they will always be depressed and gloomy.

There is only one way for the melancholy to be happy in life – focus on perfection – Jesus Christ and His Word (1 Pet. 2:21-22; Heb. 8:6-13). Where everything else in the world is flawed, our Lord and His covenant are not. This is the only way a melancholy can find true contentment in an imperfect world (Phil. 4:11). The apostle Paul penned, *"Therefore, since we have been justified by faith, we have peace with God through our Lord Jesus Christ"* (Romans 5:1). If you have Jesus in your life you have perfection in your soul (1 Jn. 3:5).

I believe Elijah was a classic melancholy; in fact, many of the prophets are believed to be of this temperament. They had a desire to relay the message of God without washing it down. They were not always popular, but the truth was more important. In fact, they were willing to die for their principles. Elijah was certainly a good example of what sometimes happens with this personality type. He had just defeated the prophets of Baal on Mount Carmel, convincing a group of confused

Israelites that God is the only true God, and brought hope during the wicked reign of Ahab and Jezebel. But all of a sudden perfection turned to chaos when Jezebel threatened his life (1 Kings. 19:2). Remember, Elijah had just witnessed the great power of God over the prophets of Baal by sending fire from heaven, but then things did not go as planned. No doubt the prophet felt like the king and queen would resign their wicked position with the hopes godliness would return to the land. But in an imperfect world, a person like Jezebel, will continue to do their evil works. Elijah became depressed. It was such a deep depression that he asked Jehovah to take his life (1 Kings. 19:4). God did not kill him nor did he have Jezebel murdered (not yet – 2 Kings. 9:30-37). Instead, the Lord treated his depression with gentleness. He allowed Elijah to get some rest and sent an angel to take care of him (1 Kings. 19:5-8). He was led to Mount Sinai, the mountain of God, where he witnessed a great windstorm, earthquake, and fire that announced the arrival of God. All of a sudden Elijah heard the gentle whisper of the Lord (1 Kings. 19:11-12). The lesson for the melancholy is that God is sometimes quietly doing His work in our lives. When all seems chaotic He tells us to listen humbly for His quiet voice in the world. Elijah was still living in an imperfect world, but now he was reminded that he had a perfect Father to care for him. This is all the perfection a melancholy truly needs in a world like ours.

PESSIMISTIC

The melancholy is a very intelligent person. They like details, fact, and figures. They have a unique ability to analyze any given situation and make sound conclusions. However, when the numbers do not add up on their calculators or fit into their pie charts they can become very pessimistic. They sometimes replace faith in God with "being realistic." Wasn't this part of Elijah's problem? He looked around at the situation and said, *"I, even I only, am left, and they seek my life, to take it away"* (1 Kings 19:10,14). Elijah had seen his nation's leaders and even the priesthood become corrupt, and felt that he was the only one left following God. Looking at the current situation it seemed *realistic* to feel this way. However, he had forgotten an elemental key to the equation – God.

There were some things that Elijah did not know about, such as, the 7,000 in Israel who had not bowed down to Baal (1 Kings 19:18). The point is this, sometimes we do not know all the facts because God is testing our faith. The Hebrew writer said, *"Now faith is the assurance of things hoped for, the conviction of things not seen"* (Heb. 11:1). It was the ten *realists* that said Canaan could not be conquered (Num. 13:28-29). It was 22,000 *realists* who said 32,000 men could not defeat 135,000 Midianites and went home (Jdgs. 7:3), although it only took 300 faithful men to bring them down (7:15-25). It was group of *realistic* disciples who counted their money and decided there were not enough funds to feed over 5,000 people (Mk. 6:37). Thomas was *realistic* in doubting the resurrection of Christ, it wasn't like he had seen nail prints in his hands (Jn. 20:25). Realistically they were right, but as a matter of faith, they were wrong.

God does not handle things in a realistic way; in fact, there is no need for God if we expect things to happen as we calculate them. This is why we need a Savior in the world, a Father we can call out to, and a Spirit we can trust. It is unrealistic to think a mighty wall would crumble by the marching and shouting of an army, but it happened (Josh. 6:20). It was unrealistic for young David to think he could bring down a giant warrior, but he did (I Sam. 17:49). It is pretty unrealistic to think we can have our sins taken way and forgotten, but it happens through God as well (Acts 2:38). With God unrealistic odds become realistic (Rom. 8:37).

The church must be careful of the pessimistic melancholy members sitting in the pews. These are the brethren who think the impossible is impossible. They will make statements like, "It can't be done," "We don't have the money to minister to others," or "Our community is impossible to evangelize." Have you ever heard these statements coming from the mouths of brothers and sisters in Christ? The melancholy has to learn to let go and allow God to work His power in the church. The apostle Paul wrote to the Corinthians that *"your faith might not rest in the wisdom of men but in the power of God"* (1 Cor. 2:5).

LOW SELF-IMAGE

This may be the most difficult to understand of all the weaknesses of the temperaments. The melancholy possesses more talent and ability of them all, but struggles with negative thinking patterns. If you notice, all their strengths and weaknesses are linked to their thoughts. They have a difficult time dealing with criticism and will overanalyze people's statements to them. For example, a melancholy can approach someone and ask them how they are doing, if they reply "fine" and walk off, they may take that to mean this person is upset with them. Or if they are walking toward a group of people and hear them whispering or laughing, they can automatically assume it is about them. This would be overanalyzing a situation that leads to a low self-image.

Yet, Christians should have a healthy self-image about themselves, not arrogant, but self-assured. Our value comes from God (Gen. 2:7), who gives us our life and worth. Luke 12:7 says *"Why even the hairs of your head are all numbered. Fear not; you are of more value than many sparrows."* Jesus said our value is how God views us, not others or even ourselves. The world judges us on how we perform, achieve, and look, but God cares for us because we belong to Him. Sometimes we need to remind ourselves of God's grace. The Father does not love us for our works (Eph. 2:4-9) or talents (Matt. 25:15). He loves us unconditionally simply because we are His children (Rom. 8:6).

Melvin and Melissa Melancholy are wonderful creations of God, but without Christ they are powerless. No one needs the mind of Christ more than this temperament.

CHAPTER 4

MEET THE CONGREGATION

Phil and Phyllis Phlegmatic - The Peacemaker

This is the last of the four temperaments. The phlegmatic introvert is a quiet person who is rarely noticed in a room full of people, and that is the way they like it. They are the easiest personality to get along with in the church. Let's think of them as a old style VW Bug, laid back and easy to deal with.

PHLEGMATIC POSITIVES

PEACEMAKER

If there were only one thing the Phlegmatic could offer the church, bringing peace would be the ideal. This is a constant theme throughout the Scriptures. According to the King James Version of the Bible the word *peace* is used over 400 times; *peaceable* is used 8 times; *peaceably* 12 times; and *peacemakers* once. This was the standard greeting of the apostle Paul in his letters to the early churches (i.e. Rom.

1:7). The Good News of Jesus Christ is called the *gospel of peace* (Rom. 10:15), and every member of the Godhead bears the nature of peace (Jn. 14:27; Gal. 5:22; Phil. 4:9).

Peace is a trait that every Christian should strive for, especially since *"God has called you to peace"* (1 Cor. 7:15). Paul wrote, *"so far as it depends on you, live peaceably with all"* (Rom. 12:18). In the Sermon on the Mount, Jesus instructed *"Blessed are the peacemakers, for they shall be called sons of God"* (Matt. 5:9). The New Living Translation puts it this way, *"God blesses those who work for peace."* These are the bridge builders in the church. They try to maintain peace with those around them. If there is a conflict they are quick to mediate various problems between Christians. They are able to keep their heads and find a point of agreement, where the other temperaments are tempted to lash out or crawl into a shell.

The church is made up of varying personalities, genders, and backgrounds that will always create tension. We all have opinions that we value. Therefore we will always have disagreements in the church. We must learn to communicate in a proper way; to disagree without being disagreeable; and speak to one another in love (Eph. 4:15). The phlegmatic has a unique way of dealing with conflict. We are to settle our differences with each other (Phil. 4:2-3). This is why the peacemaker is so important to the church.

A great example of the peacemaking phlegmatic is found in 1 Samuel 25 in a woman named Abigail. She was a beautiful and sensible woman (v. 3). She was probably the best woman her husband, Nabal, could afford, yet he took her for granted. At this point David is still on the run from King Saul, and moved near this wealthy family.

Nabal had 3,000 sheep and 1,000 goats, and when the story took place, it was sheep shearing time (v. 4). David sent ten of his men to Nabal to tell him he had been protecting his flock (vs. 15,16), and to ask him to compensate his men for their good deeds (vs. 5-9). According to the customs of the day, hospitality demanded that travelers be fed. Nabal was a very rich man and could have afforded to feed all 600 of David's men. However, Nabal arrogantly refused (vs. 10-12). This made David angry and he rounded up a posse of 400 men to ride down to murder Nabal (v. 13). Meanwhile, one of Nabal's servants told Abigail about her husband's insults to David and his men. She immediately went into action loading up huge amounts of food to take to him (v. 18).

Nabal did not know what was going on. He had been partying and getting drunk (v. 36). Abigail knew he would disapprove, but she was being a peacemaker. When she rode out to meet David's men she jumped off her donkey and humbly bowed down to him (v. 23). Just like a good peacemaker, she started smoothing things over by referring to her husband as wicked and ill tempered. Then she pleaded to David, that had she known his servants had come she would have taken care of things (vs. 24,25). In verse 26 she began thanking him for saving Nabal's life before David had any time to speak. Next she asked for his forgiveness if she offended him in any way, knowing she had not (v. 28). It is fascinating the way Abigail changed the subject, going from Nabal's sin to David's future kingship (v. 29-31). By the time she gets finished with David he is thanking God for keeping him from murdering Nabal (v. 32-34). Nabal didn't deserve such loyalty, but Abigail was a peacemaker. David would eventually add her as a wife after Nabal died, ten days later.

We need peacemakers in the church – those who work for peace even when others do not deserve it.

HUMBLE

The phlegmatic has found the key to greatness and success. This is an interesting statement to make about a non-aggressive personality. When we think of achievement and glory, the phlegmatic counterpart comes to mind – the choleric. Yet, Jesus said the key to true greatness is humility. Matthew 5:3 says, *"Blessed are the poor in spirit, for theirs is the kingdom of heaven."* This is speaking of those with deep humility. Jesus taught: *"But whoever would be great among you must be your servant"*

(Matthew 20:26). The world gives a different philosophy – dominate and take charge.

It is natural for the phlegmatic to assume a lowly station in life. They are very content to let others have their way. They find greater joy in serving than being served. Paul tried to teach the church this lesson (Phil. 2:3, 4).

Two of the most watched and anticipated funerals of our time were "Mother" Teresa of Calcutta and Princess Diana. Why did the world have such a fascination for these women? It was not because of their personal accomplishments – "Mother" Teresa had no money or things to speak of and Princess Diana, while rich, was not known for her business successes. They were loved and known for their servant hearts. Both did good works for others and the world loved them for their dedication. When Donald Trump or Bill Gates dies, their deaths will be national news, but it will not cause the world to stop and mourn. Your fortunes and achievements die with you, but respect lives forever (Ps. 49:16,17).

One of the most respected phlegmatic personalities of the Bible is Mary of Bethany. She was the sister of Martha and Lazarus. Jesus said her humble acts would be remembered wherever the gospel is preached (Matt. 26:13). Yet, the only time Mary is recorded saying anything, was when she repeated the complaint of Martha (Lk. 11:32). Just like a phlegmatic, Mary said very little. She had poured expensive perfumed oil over Jesus' head and his feet – she didn't have to say anything. In Luke 10:38-41, we find Mary humbly sitting at the feet of Jesus, again being still and quiet. The greatest work in the world is not accomplished by the best speakers, but those with the greatest humility. The Christian phlegmatic uses few words and has a humble heart.

Humility is the qualification that will lead to God (Jms. 4:6,10). We need this kind of attitude in the church. How many church splits could have been avoided with humility? How many more good works could have been accomplished with more phlegmatic members?

PATIENT

The Scriptures have a lot to say about patience. The word itself refers to the endurance of outward circumstances. The Biblical word *"long-suffering"* refers more to enduring difficult people. This can be difficult for most personalities, but this is a virtue among phlegmatics.

I used to play tennis with a church member that was a dominant phlegmatic in his mid-twenties. When you play like I do, it is great to have this temperament as a partner. My hitting bad shots, double faulting a serve or just being out of breath did not cause him to get upset with my play. I could single handedly lose a game and it wouldn't bother him. If this had been a dominant choleric they would have rolled their eyes, made deep sighing sounds of frustration, maybe even yelled a few times. The phlegmatic has a unique ability to stay calm in difficult situations.

The church needs this type of personality. 2 Timothy 2:24, *"And the Lord's servant must not be quarrelsome but kind to everyone… patiently enduring evil."* Paul was giving Timothy advice in handling those who were confused about the teachings of the church. Do we ever get impatient and frustrated with new converts? Paul says be patient and avoid foolish and ignorant questions that start fights (v. 23).

Patience is the way to understanding (Prov. 14:29), experience (Rom. 5:3,4), and the promises of God (Heb. 10:36).

PHLEGMATIC NEGATIVES

APATHETIC

The phlegmatic is not an overly enthusiastic temperament and can give the idea that Christianity is dull and lifeless. There can be a lack of emotion in spiritual things. It is not that they reject Christ and His teachings, but they do not seem enthusiastic about their spiritual zeal. Christianity is an exciting religion and should be displayed with zeal. Colossians 3:23, says, *"Whatever you do, work heartily, as for the*

Lord and not for men." In Galatians 4:18 Paul writes *"It is always good to be made much of for a good purpose…"*

Timothy seems a great example of a Phlegmatic and often displayed a lack of enthusiasm. We know of his many positive phlegmatic traits. We know he was faithful (Phil. 2:22), compassionate (Phil. 2:20; 1 Thess. 3:2), well liked (Acts 16:2), submissive (Acts 16:3), and a peacemaker (1 Cor. 4:17). His name is mentioned in 13 New Testament books; he accompanied Paul on his second missionary journey; signed his name (along side of Paul) in five New Testament books (2 Cor. 1:1; Phil. 1:1; Col. 1:1; I and 2 Thess. 1:1); and had two personal letters sent to him from the apostle Paul (1 and 2 Timothy). But what do we really know about Timothy? Why isn't he remembered like Paul? He was a phlegmatic and maintained a reserved nature. It appears that part of the purpose of the books of first and second Timothy was written to light a fire under him (1 Tim. 1:18; 6:11-20; 2 Tim. 1:6-8; 2:1-13; 4:1-5). These letters were written toward the end of Paul's life (2 Tim. 4:7). They were letters to encourage, comfort, and direct Timothy. Every phlegmatic struggling with apathy should read these books often.

PROCRASTINATOR

If the phlegmatic isn't careful patience can turn into procrastination. Their easygoing manner can prevent them from doing anything. Due to their lack of enthusiasm, they can have difficultly finding anything worth getting in a hurry over.

This can pose a great problem in the church, because important visits will be forgotten, works will be left undone, and souls will be lost. The results of procrastination are costly (Matt. 25:2-13; Acts 24:25; Prov. 27:1). Ecclesiastes 11:4 says *"He who observes the wind will not sow, and he who regards the clouds will not reap."* Paul reminded Timothy *"This charge I entrust to you, Timothy, my child, in accordance with the prophecies previously made about you, that by them you may wage the good warfare"* (1 Tim. 1:18). In 5:12 he says *"Fight the good fight of faith."* Don't delay Timothy – get in the fight. In 1 Timothy 4:14, Paul encourages him to *"not neglect the gift you have, which was given you by prophecy when the council of elders laid their hands on you."*

The phlegmatic must stop making excuses and get busy doing the Lord's work.

INTERNALIZE EMOTIONS

The phlegmatics, because of the need to be at peace with the world, will often bottle up their emotions. This is not a problem with the extrovert personalities of the sanguine and choleric, but for introverts it can pose a problem. This can lead to physical and emotional pain.

Timothy struggled with internal issues. Paul alludes to some of the stresses of ministry when he says *"Let no one despise you for your youth…"* (1 Tim. 4:12). He is straight with Timothy as he writes, *"in the last days there will come times of difficulty"* (2 Tim. 3:1). 2 Timothy 4:4 he is told to *"endure suffering, do the work of an evangelist, fulfill your ministry."* This creates an enormous amount of internal issues for the phlegmatic because they do not like conflict. I believe this is why Timothy is having stomach issues. Paul had told him *"No longer drink only water, but use a little wine for the sake of your stomach and your frequent ailments"* (1 Tim. 5:23). The text does not reveal the nature of his pain, but I believe Timothy may have been dealing with some stress-related issues. There was a lot for this phlegmatic to internalize – false teachers (1 Tim. 1:20; 2 Tim. 2:17); those who had been following the teachings of Greek philosophers (1 Tim. 4:1-8); and the people who wanted to cause conflict and arguments (1 Tim. 6:3-5, 20; 2 Tim. 2:14-16, 23). Timothy was young, according to that day and age and was dealing with a lot of people who would have tried to take advantage of him. Imagine a poor minister telling the rich to stop trusting in their riches.

What were these stomach problems? They could have been indigestion triggered by emotional stress. Research shows that stomach issues are often related to upsetting situations, such as conflict. Our emotions play a major role in our digestive health. It is doubtful this is an ulcer, since Paul prescribed *a little wine*. But doctors do encourage such for indigestion problems. I am not suggesting a phlegmatic take up drinking. The ancient Persians, Egyptians, Babylonians, and

Chinese prescribed such for their medicines. The issue is the stress that Timothy was feeling and the problems he was facing in ministry.

The phlegmatic in a leadership position must be careful in how they handle stress. They need to learn to vent and have someone they can talk with about the things they are going through. How many times have we been surprised to learn that quiet natured individual had a stroke, heart attack, or other physical problems? We often say, "They didn't seem stressed." Internalization can be deadly.

Phil and Phyllis Phlegmatic are a wonderful couple in the church. We need them to maintain peace and harmony. However, as we have seen, even this positive personality carried to extremes can be hurtful to others and especially to the phlegmatic person.

CHAPTER 5

THE MASTER PERSONALITY

The Temperament of Jesus

When Immanuel came to the earth He set the perfect standard of what man should aspire to be. As Peter penned *"For to this you have been called, because Christ also suffered for you, leaving you an example, so that you might follow his steps"* (1 Pet. 2:21). John put it this way *"whoever says he abides in him ought to walk in the same way in which he walked"* (1 Jn. 2:6). We get the spiritual meaning behind these verses, but does this also include personality? It may more than you would think.

The first thing we need to determine is the temperament of Christ. The easy answer is that Jesus perfectly reflected all of them – all of the strengths and none of the weaknesses. Therefore to become like Christ we must develop the strengths of the personalities and do away with those weaknesses. This is not about taking away your unique traits, but when you begin to eliminate your weaknesses you gain the strengths of the other personalities. More importantly we become more like Jesus.

THE SANGUINE SAVIOR

LIFE

A group of Sadducees came up to Jesus to question Him on marriage and its function in heaven. Jesus tells them something of His sanguine personality when He said *"He is not the God of the dead, but of the living"* (Matt. 22:32). Jesus always viewed others alive and full of possibilities.

When Jesus entered a room, people could feel the electricity. Think about the account of Jesus riding into Jerusalem on a colt (Matt. 21:1-11). The crowds spread out their coats on the road and cut branches from trees and placed them along the path. People lined the streets shouting *"Hosanna to the Son of David! Blessed is he who comes in the name of the Lord!"* (v. 9). The city was *stirred* by His presence (v. 10). This was not the common reception Jesus received, but there are many times the Scriptures indicate this energy and life He reflected from His presence (Matt. 9:19-21; Mk. 3:7-9; Lk. 7:36-38; Jn. 6:1-5).

Jesus described Himself as the life of the world. He is the *bread of life* (Jn. 6:35), *light* (Jn. 9:5), *the true vine* (Jn. 15:1,4), *the resurrection and the life* (Jn. 11:25,26), and the *Alpha and the Omega* (Rev. 22:13). These are all metaphors for life and energy. When Paul addressed the men of Areopagus he said *"In him we live and move and have our being"* (Acts 17:28). 1 John 5:12 says *"Whoever has the Son has life."* Jesus came to give us life (Jn. 10:10), and this is one of the great positives of the sanguine personality.

MOTIVATOR

Jesus had an incredible ability to motivate others to follow Him. That has not diminished in two thousand years. He inspired Peter, Andrew, James and John to leave their commercial fishing company to join Him in His ministry (Matt. 4:18-22). He encouraged Matthew to leave his lucrative tax business to follow Him (Matt. 9:9). All of the apostles left their homes and businesses to do the work of the Lord. They were not promised great riches or a higher-ranking position. Instead,

Jesus told them: *"take nothing for (your) journey except a staff – no bread, no bag, no money in their belts- but to wear sandals and not put on two tunics"* (Mk. 6:8-9).

Many people give up their lives, their homes, and endure countless persecutions to follow Jesus (Acts 8:1-3). No other figure in the history of the world has motivated so many for such a great length of time.

FRIENDLY

The sanguine is the friendliest of all temperaments, and this definitely describes the nature of Jesus. Our Lord was friendly to all, regardless of race (Jn. 4:7-9), sin (Jn. 8:3-11), or background (Matt. 8:5-13). In fact, He was known as the *friend of sinners* (Lk. 7:34). People were constantly coming to Christ. He was friendly and approachable (Matt. 8:2,5; 9:18; 9:27; 14:36; 15:22, 30; 17:14,15; 19:13). Even children wanted to be around Him. This is the same relationship that Christ calls all Christians to have toward one another (Jn. 15:12-17; Rom. 16:16), and to the lost (I Jn. 4:8).

Jesus was kind and friendly to people who had never received such in their lives. This was the way to people's hearts, and this is the way to the lost world today. This is the sanguine Savior.

THE CHOLERIC CHRIST

SUCCESSFUL

There is not one thing about the life of Christ that wasn't a success. Not that everyone who met Him became a follower (Matt. 8:34; 9:34; Jn. 11:38-46). Still, none of His plans ever failed. Followers of Christ in the 21st Century are living proof of His success (Matt. 16:18; Dan. 2:44). Jesus' plan to launch His church into all the world has been achieved (Acts 1:8).

Thanks to our Savior, we too can be a success in life. We may never build a great company, live in the most luxurious house, or compete in the Olympics, but with Christ we will be successful. *"For you know the grace of our Lord Jesus Christ, that though he was rich, yet for your sake he became poor, so that you by his poverty might become rich"* (2 Cor. 8:9). Christians are rich in forgiveness, joy, peace, and glory. We are joint heirs with Christ (Rom. 8:17).

LEADER

The greatest leader of all times was not Napoleon Bonaparte, Martin Luther King, General Douglas MacArther, or any worldly king or president. The greatest leader of all times was/is Jesus Christ of Nazareth. One of the most unique books I have ever found on the leadership of Christ, entitled, *Jesus CEO* by Laurie Beth Jones I bought from Office Depot. It was written for businessmen and women on how to be a successful executive through the leadership qualities of Christ. It truly shows Jesus in His full choleric form, pointing out his strengthens in self-mastery, action, and relationships. The back cover reads: "Following the example of Jesus – a 'CEO' who took a disorganized 'staff' of twelve and built a thriving enterprise." Not exactly how the Bible describes it, but interesting. Jesus really did take a group of men, with differing backgrounds, personalities and occupations, and use them to help spread His message to the entire world (Matt. 28:19,20).

We need leaders like Jesus in our world and especially in the church. A choleric can learn to perfect leadership qualities by observing Christ.

PERSISTENT

Jesus declared: *"For I have come down from heaven, not to do my own will but the will of him who sent me"* (Jn. 6:38). This was His mission and He never lost focus of that goal. Even when He was being tempted by Satan (Matt. 4:1-11); ridiculed by His brothers (Jn. 7:1-5); tested by the Scribes and Pharisees (Matt. 12:9-13); learned that His cousin John had been beheaded (Matt. 14:10-13); agonized in the Garden of Gethsemane (Matt. 26:36-44); was betrayed by one of His own (Mk. 14:43-52); was questioned by Caiaphas (Matt. 26:57-68); denied by Thomas (Lk. 22:54-65); stood before Pilate (Mk. 15:1-5); was rejected by His people for a criminal (Matt. 27:15-26); mocked by the Roman soldiers (Mk. 15:16-20); nailed to a cross (Matt. 27:35); or separated from the Father (Jn. 19:28-37), Jesus persisted in doing the will of God.

This is the kind of persistence every Christian needs to complete their spiritual journey on earth. Life is not always easy, especially if you are a Christian (II Tim. 3:12). We need the persistence of Christ.

THE MELANCHOLY MESSIAH

ANALYTICAL

No one could match wits with the Messiah. Jesus was a thinker and proved His powerful analytical mind several times while dealing with the Scribes and Pharisees. Once when Jesus and His disciples were walking through a grain field, they began breaking off heads of grain to eat, because they were hungry. Some Pharisees saw them and told Jesus that what His men were doing was unlawful because it violated the Sabbath laws of working on this holy day. His response: *"Have you not read what David did when he was hungry, and those who were with him: how he entered the house of God and ate the bread of the Presence, which it was not lawful for him to eat nor for those who were with him, but only for the priests? Or have you not read in the Law how on the Sabbath the priests in the temple profane the Sabbath and are guiltless?"* (Matt. 12:3-5). His answer proved that the Sabbath laws did not restrict deeds of necessity, service to God, or acts of mercy (v. 7,8). Actually, there wasn't a law prohibiting the breaking off of grain and eating on the Sabbath (Deut. 23:25). Taking a handful of grain from a neighbor's field to satisfy hunger was permitted. The Pharisees had established 39 different categories of things forbidden on the Sabbath, based on their Jewish traditions. Jesus proved that this day was set up for man's benefit and God's glory and not a law of bondage (Mk. 2:27). The Pharisees gave no room for compassion.

On another occasion the Scribes accused Jesus of getting His power from Satan, since he could cast out demons (Mk. 3:20 30). Jesus responded by saying *"How can Satan cast out Satan? If a kingdom is divided against itself, that kingdom cannot stand. And if a house is divided against itself, that house will not be able to stand. And if Satan has risen up against himself and is divided, he cannot stand, but is coming to an end"* (v. 23-26). In other words, their reasoning was foolish and didn't make sense.

These are only a couple of examples of the amazing analytical abilities of Christ. Not everyone will have the natural logical reasoning of the melancholy, but through study and the Scriptures we are given the knowledge we need to answer questions about our faith (1 Pet. 3:15).

ORGANIZED

Everything Jesus did had been planned out and organized before His coming to the earth (Eph. 1:5). The prophets spoke about the plans of His coming (Isa. 53); His ministry was prepared and announced through John the Baptizer (Matt. 3:2,3); Jesus organized the disciples by sending them out two by two (Mk. 6:7), and would eventually use them to send His message of repentance and salvation to the world (Acts 2). Jesus strategically placed Paul in a position to reach the Gentiles and other people of influence (Acts 9:15; Rom. 11:13; 15:16). He organized elders and deacons to be appointed among these newly founded churches of Christ (1 Tim. 3:1-13). Everything He did was perfectly planned and organized.

Organization should not just be for the melancholy but every member of the church (1 Cor. 14:40).

COMPASSIONATE

The melancholy has a compassionate and tender heart. This is a strong trait of Jesus Christ.

The Biblical meaning of *compassion* comes from the Greek word *splanchnizomai*, meaning "to be moved as to one's inwards (*splanchna*), to be moved with compassion, to yearn with compassion." It is a verb derived from *splanchna* meaning "the inward parts," more especially the heart, lungs, liver, and kidneys. Those body parts represent the seat of the affections, as we often use the word *heart*. It is our deepest emotion towards others. It is a great word that even describes the feelings God has for mankind (Jn. 3:16).

Jesus set the example for the compassion of God. In Matthew 15:32, Jesus had *compassion on the crowd*, which was an occasion when a group of lame, blind, crippled, mute, and many others with physical ailments, came to Jesus to be healed. For three days these people waited and listened to their Messiah. All the while, the crowds grew in excess to about 4,000. On one occasion two blind men were sitting beside the road when they received word that Jesus was coming their way. They immediately began to shout out to Him. Even though He was nearing the end of the line, as He was drawing nearer to Jerusalem, He *had compassion* on the men and healed them (Matt. 20:32-34). Jesus was *moved with pity* over the faith and humility of a leper (Mk. 1:41), and *had compassion* on a widow who was having to bury her only son (Lk. 7:13).

On another occasion Jesus was looking out over Jerusalem and with compassion said *"O Jerusalem, Jerusalem, the city that kills the prophets and stones those who are sent to it! How often would I have gathered your children together your children together as a hen gathers her brood under her wings, and you were not willing!"* (Matt. 23:37). In no greater way do we see the sympathy of Christ over the world than in the cross. Our Lord desires good for all men, not evil, and grieves over the lost (2 Pet. 3:9). *Jesus wept* (Jn. 11:35) over the unbelief of man. It is the same deep-seated compassion He expresses to the world today. This is the same compassion we must have for the lost. Not everyone will choose to serve Christ, but our compassionate hearts must continually go out to them (1 Pet. 3:8).

THE PHLEGMATIC PRINCE OF PEACE

PEACEFUL

The prophet Isaiah referred to Jesus as the *Prince of Peace* (Isa. 9:6). At His birth the angels shouted, *"Glory to God in the highest, and on earth peace among those with whom he is pleased!"* (Lk. 2:14). This was not a cry for world peace, but to have peace with God, which comes through Jesus Christ (Rom. 5:1). Unlike world peace (which usually means no conflict), the peace of Christ was a calm assurance of the future. It is a gift He left with us (Jn. 14:27; 16:33). The apostle Paul said *"he himself is our peace"* (Eph. 2:14). This is an inner confidence that everything is going to work out despite our outward circumstances (Rom. 8:28). Rather than allowing the stresses of life to get you down, allow the Prince of Peace to give you a calming assurance. His purpose was to bring a greater, more peaceful law – the law of Christ.

Jesus worked for peace, whether it was a raging storm (Mk. 4:39), conflict between his own disciples (Matt. 18:1-6), or potential bloodshed (Jn. 8:2-11; Matt. 26:51-53).

HUMBLE

The humility of Jesus is one of the most unique qualities of God, as well as one of the most difficult to understand. Think about it, Christ the Creator, spoke the universe into existence (Jn. 1:3,10; Eph. 3:9; Col. 1:16), holds His creation together by the mighty power of His word (Heb. 1:3), and maintains the power of eternal life in His hands (Jn. 1:4). The winds and the sea obey Him (Matt. 8:27), demons fear Him (Jms. 2:19), and angels worship Him (Heb. 1:6). Christ is God! God is Christ! John the Baptizer spoke of His greatness when he said he wasn't worthy of being His slave (Matt. 3:11). Paul would later write: *"Therefore God has highly exalted him and bestowed on him the name that is above every name, so that at the name of Jesus every knee should bow, in heaven and on earth and under the earth"* (Phil. 2:9,10). Then we learn of the humility of Christ: *"Who, though he was in the form of God, did not count equality with God a thing to be grasped, but emptied himself, by taking the form of a servant, being born in the likeness of men"* (Phil. 2:6,7) God is humble and Jesus came to show us what that means (Jn. 13:14). Why? This is the way to God (1 Pet. 5:5,6).

PATIENT

Peter said *"..with the Lord one day is as a thousand years, and a thousand years as one day. The lord is not slow to fulfill his promise as some count slowness, but is patient toward you"* (2 Pet. 3:8,9). This is another personality trait of God. Where would we be without the Lord's patience? Jesus demonstrated this attribute while He walked the earth in bodily form. He had the power to take the life of another by a mere thought, and yet patiently endured the false accusations of the Scribes and Pharisees (even while they accused Him of being from Satan – Matt. 12:24). As a strong choleric I would have wanted to make at least one example out of those religious leaders. Who hasn't entertained the thought of punching Judas in the nose when he betrayed Jesus with a kiss (Mk. 14:43-52), or sending electric shock through the body of those soldiers who mocked Him (Matt. 27:27-31)? Maybe not kill them or hurt them too bad, but at least put fear in them by pinning them to the ceiling of the Temple. Jesus did none of these things. He was only concerned with those who believed in Him.

I need the phlegmatic patience of Christ.

Jesus was the Master personality. He had all the struggles and none of the temperament weaknesses. If we aspire to be like Him the study of the personalities will help us.

CHAPTER 6

YOU ARE SPECIAL

Developing your Personality

For you formed my inward parts;
  you knitted me together in my mother's womb.
I praise you, for I am fearfully and wonderfully made.
  Wonderful are your works;
    my soul knows it very well.
My frame was not hidden from you,
when I was being made in secret,
  intricately woven in the depths of the earth.
Your eyes saw my unformed substance;
In your book were written, every one of them,
  The days that were formed for me,
  When as yet there was none of them. (Psalm 139:13-16)

The distinctive elements of God have been carefully given to mankind in creation. The word *inward* comes from a Hebrew word *kilyah*, which literally means "kidney (as an essential organ); figuratively the *mind* (as the interior self)." The Hebrews considered the kidneys as the seat of emotions and desires. This would include the passions and desires of the personalities. Therefore God *fearfully and wonderfully* created each of us with distinctive temperaments.

This chapter is to help you discover these magnificent traits. This is important as many try to be like someone else; thinking the other personality is better than their own. This isn't to say we do not have weaknesses that need to be eliminated, but neither should we desire to be someone God has not designed us to be.

YOU ARE SPECIAL

YOU WERE CREATED BY GOD

As David revealed in Psalm 139, we are special because God created us. The works of God are *great* (Ps. 92:5). If you were born a sanguine, choleric, melancholy, or phlegmatic, you are distinctive in nature. You were not created by a great scientist or developed from an ape – you were created and designed by God.

You may never develop a life-saving cure, serve as the President of the United States, or win a Pulitzer Prize, but you can say the One who gives eternal life, is petitioned by the highest offices in the world, and formed the great thinkers of our time – created you. If that doesn't make you special, nothing will.

YOU WERE CREATED OUT OF LOVE

Karen Cogan tells a story about a young boy coming home from Vacation Bible School with his mom. As they rode in the car little Timothy started humming the song "Jesus Loves Me, This I Know." At one point he stopped singing and asked his mother if God really loved him. She quickly replied, "Oh yes, God loves you very much." As any persistent child would do he asked her why he loved him. Timothy's mom pointed to the picture he had drawn in Vacation Bible School, with flowers, grass, and trees, and asked him why that picture was special to him. His response, "I made it." His mother nodded and said, "It's like that with God, He loves us because he made us."

Job questioned his creation, during those horrific physical and mental trials, by saying,

Your hands fashioned and made me,
  And now you have destroyed me altogether.
Remember that you have made me like clay;
  and you will return to me to the dust?
Did you not pour me out like milk
  and curdle me like cheese?
You clothed me with skin and flesh,
  and knit me together with bones and sinews. (Job 10:8-11)

Then He ends with a unique statement: *"You granted me life and steadfast love"* (v. 12). God proved His love by exchanging the life of sinful man for the life of His Perfect Son (Jn. 3:16). Your personality was created out of an unconditional love for man. This study only enhances His affection for us.

YOU WERE CREATED WITH GENUINE WORTH
Listen to the words David penned in Psalm 8:3-8,

When I look at your heavens, the work of your fingers,
  the moon and the stars, which you have set in place,
what is man that you are mindful of him,
  and the son of man that you care for them?

Yet you have made him a little lower than the heavenly begins
  and crowned him with glory and honor.
You have given him dominion over the works of your hands;
  you have put all things under his feet,
all sheep and oxen,
  and also the beasts of the field,

the birds of the heavens, and the fish of the sea,
  whatever passes along the paths of the seas.

When we compare ourselves to the Creator, we will begin to see God in His awesome holiness. It humbles us, or at least it should. Think about it, if the entire universe is tiny in comparison to its Divine Creator, *what is man?* As one commentator put it, "When we look at the vast, seemingly endless universe and then think about the little dot that we call earth in the middle of it all, we, too, cannot but ask, 'What is man? What right do we have to be so much in the mind of God?'" Even the Hebrew word *enosh,* translated "man," signifies the weakness of man rather than his strength.

It is important for creation to put things into perspective with the Creator. Yet, these verses were not intended to make us feel worthless, but to understand our true value. Even though we are inferior to God He *crowned* us with *glory and honor.* David is proclaiming our worth to the Almighty. He placed us over everything He created. This place wasn't given to the angels, instead they are to minister to those who receive salvation (Heb. 1:14). God exalted us in His creation. We were created with genuine worth, not of our own, but of God's. Your personality is just one of the special ways He gave us value.

IN HIS IMAGE

Then God said, "Let us make man in our image, after our likeness. And let them have dominion over the fish of the sea and over the birds of the heavens and over the livestock and over all the earth and over every creeping thing that creeps on the earth."

  So God created man in his own image,
    in the image of God he created him;
    male and female he created them. (Gen. 1:26-27)

The question is asked, "Was I born this way?" The answer is found in the first chapter of the Bible – YES! These verses alone explain why every person and temperament is special: we are created in the image of God. That should give you a strong foundation of self-worth. Human worth is not based on the things we own, our achievements, physical beauty, or public acclaim. Our worth is based on being made in God's image. Think about this for a moment, of all of God's creation, mankind is the only one that originated from the image of God. Everything else He made was *good*, but when He created man He said it was *very good* (Gen. 1:31).

IMAGE DEFINED

Have you ever wondered what it means to be created in the image of God? It cannot refer to physical features since God is Spirit (Jn. 4:24) and we are made of flesh and bones (Gen. 2:23). The word *image* comes from the Hebrew word *tselem* to mean "likeness, resemblance; a representative figure."

God made man in such a way as to reflect some of His own perfections. The personalities, in my opinion, are one of those reflective traits of the Godhead. Our last chapter dealt with the personality of Jesus Christ, and our conclusion was the more we become like Christ the closer we come to perfection through our temperament. Following the steps of Jesus is eliminating our weaknesses and thereby gaining the strengths of the other temperament types. The personalities are only one of the ways we become more like God. The Hebrew word for image does not mean an exact replica but more of a shadow of a thing. We will never be a carbon copy of God, but we do reflect His character through our lives and personalities.

A HEAVENLY PERSPECTIVE

I believe the Bible teaches we will know one another in heaven. The Scriptures tells that Abraham, Isaac, and Jacob were joined to their ancestors at death (Gen. 25:8; 35:29; 49:33). King David was asked why he wasn't fasting and weeping over the death of his child, he responded, "*While the child was still alive, I fasted and wept, for*

I said, 'Who knows whether the Lord will be gracious to me, that the child may live?' But now he is dead. Why should I fast? Can I bring him back again? I shall go to him, but he will not return to me" (2 Sam. 12:22-23). In Matthew 17, we read of the transfiguration of Christ when Jesus leads Peter, James, and John to a high mountain to reveal His true self. Suddenly, Moses and Elijah appeared out of nowhere and began talking with Jesus. For some reason the apostles knew who they were, even though they had been dead for hundreds of years. Was there an old picture of them they had seen? Maybe some type of bust that people put on their mantles. No, somehow they knew.

When we leave this earth our physical bodies return to the dust of the earth (Gen. 3:19). Paul described it this way: *"What is sown is perishable; what is raised is imperishable. It is sown in dishonor; it is raised in glory. It is sown in weakness; it is raised in power. It is sown a natural body; it is raised a spiritual body. If there is a natural body, there is also a spiritual body"* (1 Cor. 15:42-44). There is a difference in the physical and spiritual. But then he continues, in verses 49 *"Just as we have borne the image of the man of dust, we shall also bear the image of the man of heaven."* So, if we do not retain our physical bodies in heaven, how will we know one another? In my opinion, I believe our personalities will be one of those means of retaining our identity. It is a better way than the physical because we change so much from birth until the day of our death. Personality is one of those special ways God designed us to maintain our personal characteristics.

For example, have you ever told someone a story about a person you both knew? You go through all the funny details, giving them all the specifics of what happened. After telling this mutual friend the story they respond by saying, "That sounds just like something they would do!" In other words, it fits their personality.

Or you start telling someone a story about someone else, without revealing the person you are talking about, and halfway through the story they have already figured out who you are referring too. Their personality gave them away.

Or what about those times when you are listening to a story about someone else and you turn to the person beside you and ask, "Who does that sound like to you?" Personality plays an important part of our identity.

THE PERSONALTIES OF ADAM AND EVE

Not much is given concerning the personalities of Adam and Eve. We know they were created in the image of God and are given a short episode of their fall in the Garden. Most of my theories concerning their personalities are speculations, but I believe they are sound. I believe they would have been given opposite characteristics. This would set the personalities in motion for all the descendants of Adam and Eve. In other words, Cain and Abel were given pieces of their parent's personality and their children would be given pieces of themselves, creating the mixture of every temperament type – sanguine/choleric; choleric/melancholy; melancholy/phlegmatic; phlegmatic/sanguine, etc..

Studies prove that opposites attract and likes repel. It seems God created us this way so the strengths of one spouse will provide support for the weaker nature of the other partner. For example, by nature, the sanguine (life of the party) is very disorganized; however the melancholy (the perfectionist) lives for organization. The flip side to that would be the fun-loving nature of the Sanguine helps to cheer up the depressed moods of the melancholy. Together they become stronger and more complete. Now watch this *"Then the Lord God said, 'It is not good that man should be alone; I will make him a helper fit for him'"* (Gen. 2:18). A *helper*, according to the Hebrew word *keneghdo*, means, among other things, "corresponding to, counterpart, or opposite." If God created us to marry those who are opposite from our personalities and repel those who are similar, then wouldn't it make sense that Adam and Eve were created with different personality types? The text reveals that Adam was incomplete without Eve.

If I had to guess, I would say that Eve was choleric/sanguine, and Adam was phlegmatic/melancholy. I was surprised to come to this conclusion but when you look at their fall it makes sense. Satan tempts us by using our personality weaknesses. When you read Genesis 3 we see that Satan tempted Eve with the idea of being like God, knowing everything (v. 5). This "god-syndrome" is a real weakness of the choleric (the leader). They are very determined to achieve and be successful; even it they have to eat some forbidden fruit along the way. Yet, not only did she eat some fruit but convinced Adam to do the same (v. 6), just the abilities of a sanguine who is the life of the party and doesn't want to miss out on anything. Eve wanted Adam to join in the fun. On the other hand, Adam, who had not been deceived by Satan (1 Tim. 2:14), followed the crowd, as a phlegmatic who goes along with the crowd. He did what his wife told him to do (Gen. 3:17). The phlegmatic doesn't like conflict, similar to Adam trying to hide when he hears the Lord walking in the Garden (Gen. 3:8-10). Another characteristic of Adam was his intelligence, a melancholy trait. He was placed in charge of the Garden of Eden and given the responsibility to catalogue the names of all the animals of the earth (Gen. 2:15-20).

Let's presume this is true. That being the case, their punishment would fit the personality. Strong-willed Eve would learn to be submissive to her husband (Gen. 3:16). All the sanguine fun of bearing children would be turned to sorrow at conception (Gen. 3:16). For the sluggish natured Adam, like the phlegmatic, he would be in charge of providing for his family, and it wouldn't be easy (Gen. 3:17-19). The punishment fits the personality.

CREATED FOR A PUPOSE

Have you ever wondered why God created man? Was He bored one day and decided to create a massive universe? Does God go around the universe creating planets with people as a hobby? No, the Bible says that we were brought into this world with a Divine purpose – to bring Him glory (Isa. 43:7) and pleasure (Rev. 4:11). While faith is one of the primary ingredients to please God (Heb. 11:6), our personalities aid us in bringing Him glory. Whether it is the enthusiasm of the sanguine, the leadership of the choleric, the organization of the melancholy, or the humility of the phlegmatic, we are all given special abilities to bring glory and pleasure to God.

You are *"fearfully and wonderfully made"* (Ps. 139:13), created for God's pleasure and glory. We should never wish to be someone else, because God gave us unique qualities of our own. We are special, created in His image, to bring honor to the Almighty God.

CHAPTER 7

THE FRUIT OF THE SPIRIT

Developing Your Personality

Our goal, in this study, is to build on our strengths and eliminate our weaknesses. Yet, in order to succeed, we must have the help of God. I'm going to make a case that we do this as we focus on the fruit of the Spirit being developed and grown in our lives. When we put on Christ, our temperament, along with the rest of our lives, *"become partakers of the divine nature"* (2 Pet. 1:4). While God reveals Himself in many ways (Heb. 1:1; Psa. 19:1), God's Word is the one indisputable way the Spirit guides us *"into all truth"* (Jn. 16:13). When we try to follow the example of the Bible, we will change outwardly as well as inwardly. The Holy Spirit has also worked within the conscience of man as *Helper* (Jn. 14:16), He encourages the Saints (Rom. 8:26-27). We must ultimately make the proper choices, but when the Scriptures enter our hearts the Holy Spirit dwells with it. Batsell Barrett Baxter said, "As we open our lives to the influence of God through his Word, the Holy Spirit comes to dwell within us." While there is much debate on HOW the Spirit dwells in God's saints we cannot debate THAT the Spirit guides us.

Submitting our temperament to Him is one of the ways God's Spirit enables Christians to be the people He called us to be. The fruit of the Spirit is the key to this study.

"But the fruit of the Spirit is love, joy, peace, patience, kindness, goodness, faithfulness, gentleness, self-control; against such there is no law" (Galatians 5:22-23).

THE SANGUINE - Life of the Party

PEACE

There is no personality that has as much restless energy as the sanguine. Remember our sports car all revved up and ready to go! They have short attention spans and an uneasy spirit. They constantly think about what they will be doing next. It seems some sanguines appear to have Attention Deficit Disorder. They have the ideas and charisma to succeed, but they rarely put it all together at the same time. In fact, the verb form of the word *peace* reflects the idea of "having it all together." James wrote, *"What causes quarrels and what causes fights among you? Is it not this, that your passions are at war within you?"* (Jms. 4). This is an inner battle that occurs within our souls which leads to conflict. This is why a sanguine needs the *peace* of the Spirit. This doesn't mean that one will be relieved of external conflict or inner stress, but will gain a quiet inner spirit.

In order for sanguines to enjoy this peacefulness, they must wrap their hearts with the *Prince of Peace* (Isa. 9:6). Paul wrote, *"the peace of God, which surpasses all understanding, will guard your hearts and your minds in Christ Jesus"* (Phil. 4:7). Therefore, peace comes through uniting with – *Christ Jesus*. When we are baptized into Christ we *put on Christ* (Gal. 3:27). The peace of Christ rules within our hearts (Col. 3:15).

PATIENCE

Patience or *Longsuffering* comes from a Greek word (*macrothumia*), which gives the idea of anger taking a long time to express itself. Today we often use the word patience.

It is important for Christians to develop a long-suffering attitude because there are few things in life that are as uncomfortable as being around people who lose their cool. A sanguine often reacts without thinking – lashing out before looking at the whole situation.

Growing up, I had a terrible temper as a sanguine/choleric blend. On one occasion my younger brother did something to me (as usual) and I drew back ready to hit him. Before I could do anything my mother caught me and yelled, "If you hit your brother you're going to get a spanking." I glanced at my mother and then over to my brother, weighing out the possibilities in my mind. Finally, I rared back and punched him. I turned to my mother and said, "It's worth it."

Once I became a Christian, I realized I had to submit to the Lord. It took some work, but with a new way of thinking (Rom. 12:2) I was able to overcome my temper. It did not happen overnight or through some miraculous indwelling, but through the study of God's Word and the nudging of the Spirit in my conscience. Before Christ, I did not have a true sense of right and wrong about my anger, but now self-control is a part of my everyday life. I still struggle but have better control over my emotions.

GENTLENESS

Gentleness may be better translated *meekness*. It comes from a Greek word (*prautes*) that has three basic meanings in the New Testament. One of which carries the idea of humility or literally a wild animal that has been tamed. A gentle person is easily directed by God (Col. 3:12).

Of all the temperaments, sanguines needs the humble Spirit of God. They have a tendency to talk about and think only of themselves. They interrupt others -

talking, seeking credit, and showing off in front of others. Yes, they are the life of the party, and will tell you if they get a chance.

When filled with the gentle humility of the fruit of the Spirit, attitudes change. Sanguines will no longer talk about themselves, but about Christ and His people. Their bragging will be turned upward rather than inward. Paul wrote: *"But far be it from me to boast except in the cross of our Lord Jesus Christ"* (Gal. 6:14). His pride had been turned into rejoicing over the Savior. This new attitude creates new friends and a powerful voice for God.

FAITHFULNESS

When an employer looks for employees they look for those who are committed to the job; people who are dependable, trustworthy, and responsible. The same character traits are needed in the church: people who are faithful to what they say they will do.

While sanguines are among the best volunteers in the church, they can have a problem with follow-through. Most have heard the 20/80 rule. You know, 20% of the people doing 80% of the work. Yet, a sanguine may volunteer for 100% of the work and do about 20%. Sometimes they forget about all the things they volunteered for because of their lack of organization, and sometimes they just get bored with the work at hand or find something more exciting.

This is why the sanguine needs the *faithfulness* of the Spirit. The Greek (*pistis*) signifies someone who is faithful and trustworthy; loyal and steadfast in devotion and allegiance.

SELF-CONTROL

Here is the greatest need of the sanguine. They fly from one thing to the next, without planning or organization. *Self-control* comes from a Greek word (*en kratos*) that is in reference to a person who has strength from within. They have the ability to control their desires, passions, and cravings of the flesh. One who possesses self-control has the ability to restrain his thoughts (2 Cor. 10:5), the tongue (Jms. 3:1-9), and sensual desires (1 Cor. 7:9).

The sanguine must continually call to remembrance the study concerning the instructions given us from God's Word on self-restraint. The decision is still ours, if we submit to the Spirit's control we can conquer the emotions of the flesh.

Philippians 2:13 teaches "*...it is God who works in you, both to will and to work for his good pleasure.*"

It is important to remember Sam and Samantha Sanguine will always be the colorful, fun-loving, extroverts we all fell in love with upon that first meeting. Yet, when they are guided by the Word of God, they make some noticeable changes. We begin to see the fruit of the Spirit lived out in them. Instead of making others laugh at the expense of someone else, they will restrain their words. We are not talking about changing the sanguine into a melancholy, but about enhancing their strengths by eliminating their weaknesses.

Peter is the sanguine example of this Spirit-filled transformation. He was still using his lips, but he wasn't using them to deny the Lord, but rather to preach the first gospel sermon (Acts 2:14-36). He no longer worried about what others thought of him: speaking out for Christ and adamantly preaching Jesus despite the threats of others (Acts 4:1-22). What was the difference? The Spirit of God (Acts 2:4; 4:8).

THE MELANCHOLY - The Perfectionist

LOVE

The Greek word for love (*agapè*), as used in Galatians 5:22 is the love of the mind, of the reason and will. This type of love requires a melancholy to love their neighbor (Matt. 22:39), and fellow brothers and sisters in Christ (Jn. 13:34; 15:12), regardless of whether they deserve to be loved or not. In fact, this word involves seeking the highest good for others no matter what they may do to us. It concerns the will as well as the emotions. This is not natural for the melancholy, because they feel so deeply, get offended so easily, and can harbor feelings of hurt for long periods of time. As our "smart car" they tend to learn quickly and never forget.

This is why the melancholy must have the Spirit of the Lord who instructs us to forgive others as He has forgiven us (Col. 3:13). Jesus taught that forgiving others is necessary for own forgiveness (Matt. 6:14-15). The love of God helps the melancholy to wipe away grudges and hatred toward others.

JOY

No other temperament gets depressed as easily and as often as the melancholy. This is due to their unrealistic view that the world can be perfect. They strive for perfection and end up depressed when they learn that the world is imperfect. The church is a perfect institution, but it is made up of imperfect people. Until melancholies understand the nature of mankind they will always be depressed. This is what robs them of lasting joy.

This doesn't mean Christians will go around smiling all the time, because true joy goes much deeper than that. The fruit of the Holy Spirit's joy (*chara*) is based upon the hope (1 Pet. 1:3) and promises of God (Jn. 3:16). It is a feeling of gladness that can only come from God (1 Thess. 1:6). It is more than a positive feeling, but an understanding that no matter what happens to us in life, we are in the hands of God (Acts 5:41; Jms. 1:2-3). It is delighting in Him and not in our circumstances.

PEACE

The peace (*eirene*) of God can turn the distress of the melancholy into inner calm. A worrisome nature can cause a sense of uneasiness within, but Jesus said even the melancholy can have peace in this world (Jn. 16:33). As they learn to put their trust in Christ the Spirit of God will work within their minds to give them a calming peace (Matt. 6:25, 27, 34). I always encourage distressed melancholies to read the Psalms to find spiritual peace from within (Ps. 3, 4, 6, 11, 28, 31, 46, 56, 71, 91, 102, 109, 125, 140, 142, 143, 146, etc.).

GOODNESS

The depressive attitude of the melancholy can prevent them from doing good. Goodness (*agathosune*) is not only the ability to be good and kind, but to put that kindness into action. When filled with feelings of self-pity one cannot help others. This is a different kind of selfishness from the sanguine and choleric, but self-centeredness nonetheless. If we want the Lord to hear our cries, then we must listen for others when they need kindness (Prov. 21:13).

Jesus taught us to lose our lives for others in order to save them (Lk. 17:33). The melancholy can come up with all types of excuses to get out of doing good for others. They can focus on their fears to get out of telling others about Christ, helping the poor, or getting involved in some of the works of the church. They can convince themselves that they have too many problems to get involved with other people's lives. This is a true waste of God's gifts, as they possess the greatest amount of talent. Just like the unfaithful steward, if not under the control of God, they will bury their talents in the ground (Matt. 25:14-30).

Elijah may be the perfect example of how the melancholy depression can affect their service to God. Although he had just witnessed a great victory over the prophets of Baal (1 Kgs. 18:20-40), and helped to influence the struggling Jews to put their trust in God, he was still depressed. When Elijah received word from a messenger that Jezebel was seeking his life he became severely depressed (1 Kgs. 19:1-4). No longer was his heart filled with joy and peace, but with discouragement. His deeds of goodness also ended during this time of despair. He had such an impact before, but became useless for the cause of God. However, once he was helped by the Lord and filled with God's presence (1 Kgs. 19:5-21), he was able to continue his work. The same will be the case for the depressed melancholy Christian today. The Spirit of God aids us in our work for Christ. This is why the melancholy must be filled with the fruit of the Spirit.

CHAPTER 8

THE FRUIT OF THE SPIRIT
Developing Your Personality

In our last chapter we began a study of how the fruit of the Holy Spirit aids Christians in our temperaments. Through the fruit of the Spirit, God develops personality traits found in the nature of Christ. These have to do with our reactions to the people and circumstances in life. This is more than a list of things to do or be, it is evidence that the Holy Spirit lives in us, illustrating God's personality to the world.

Galatians 5:22-23 *"But the fruit of the Spirit is love, joy, peace, patience, kindness, goodness, faithfulness, gentleness, self-control; against such things there is no law."*

THE CHOLERIC - The Leader

LOVE

God loves His people and wants them to succeed in life. He wants our business ventures to be productive (Ps. 37:29). Our Father honors those who are diligent in their work (Prov. 10:4). The choleric is the model of hard work and success. However, in their pursuit of achievements, they can also exemplify a very hard-nosed style of business. They have this killer instinct that can be financially prosperous but opposite to the nature of Christ at the same time. What they need is to grow in the Spirit of God's love (1 Jn. 4:16).

Remember love (*agape*), is the love of the mind of the reason and of the will. It means that no matter what others may do, one will never do anything but seek the highest good of others. This is a giving, self-sacrificing type of love. These traits are difficult for the choleric. But the fruit of love transforms one into the kind of person Christ exemplified on earth. It is seeing people as Jesus saw them with lenses of care and concern (Jn. 15:8-10,12).

When our focus is on success, it is easy to forget about the people we are running over to reach the goal. The love of Christ puts others over self.

This will not be an automatic response for a choleric, but with the Spirit of God we can develop a mind for others. It is a choice we make and eventually a desire. Compassion is something that can grow in our hearts toward others (1 Thess. 3:12-13).

PEACE

Just like the sanguine, the choleric needs to develop peace. All of us have had to deal with anger. Cholerics take things personally, getting upset at the slightest injustice done to them or others, and generally like for things to go their way. However, Satan's work is made up of imperfections, interruptions, and injustice. This is why the choleric must obtain the Spirit of peace.

A workaholic personality is caused, not only by a determination to succeed, but a feeling of restlessness within the soul. Again, this is where the peace of Christ needs to reign in that person's life (Phil. 4:7). It is a staying power that is able to push out inner turmoil and anxiety in life. When this happens, the peace of God will replace the inner anger of the Choleric with a peaceful contentment. Instead of letting injustice create ulcers, they will learn to turn their cares over to the Lord (1 Pet. 5:7).

PATIENCE

Another part of the fruit, which is needed in the choleric, is patience. The Greek word (*makrothumia*) does signify the "never give in" steadfast temperament, but not the same type of perseverance that is called for in the definition of the word. This type of persistence has to do with taking the attacks of others. This is the opposite of the cholerics' nature; for, they attack and defend when opposed. Which is why the personality of Christ must be manifested in their lives (Rom. 2:4).

With the help of the Spirit they will learn to endure attack rather than striking back or retaliating. It will give them the power to suffer the pressure from others.

KINDNESS

Kindness (*chrestote*) is a word that refers to a sweet disposition, considerate through all situations in life. This is a person who isn't hard, harsh, or unconcerned. It is used of old wine meaning mellow. It is care for the feelings of others.

Does this sound like the average description of a choleric personality? Not at all. In fact, the choleric temperament can be very unkind at times, especially when their control is being threatened (i.e. Diotrephes – 3 John 1:9-10).

If the choleric is to be like God, they must learn the essence of this word. Look to the Biblical display of God's goodness toward mankind (Eph. 2:4-7). It is a demonstration that should encourage us to show this attitude in our lives (Rom. 11:22). Christians are called to practice the "golden rule" (Matt. 7:12; Eph. 4:32). Many divisions in the church could be prevented with kindness of the Spirit.

GOODNESS

Goodness (*agathosune*) and kindness (*chestotes*) compliment each other. It not only means to be kind but to do kindness. Goodness is not just about what you say but your actions. It is a person who, not only is good, but does good. It is treating people as God would treat them (Mk. 10:17-18). For the choleric this can be difficult because it means this person would not take advantage of another or let others be victimized. For the dominant choleric, who is always achieving, they feel it is sometimes necessary to use others to reach their goals. However, one who is driven by goodness cannot do evil to another (Rom. 12:9).

The choleric learns this trait through the Word of God (Ps. 119:9; 2 Tim. 3:16). It teaches us how to treat our fellowman. The Spirit keeps these things present in our minds as we walk daily before others (Rom. 8:14).

GENTLENESS

Just like the sanguine, the choleric needs the gentleness of the Spirit of God. To refresh, gentleness (*prautes*) means to be tamed. It helps the Christian act in the ways of God. The choleric needs this nature because the world pushes him toward an aggressive style of leadership. Yet, Jesus taught us that leadership comes from a genuine gentleness (Prov. 13:10).

SELF-CONTROL

A choleric is a "large and in charge" kind of person. They are able to lead people to great heights and be in control of many things at the same time. However, while they are able to control their business life, they sometimes need help with their personal lives. Of all the temperaments, this one is more addicted to work than any other. In the process they will lose control over their families and sometimes their behavior. For this reason they need self-control (*egkrateia*); a control that the Spirit gives to bring balance to the activities of life (Phil. 2:13).

The apostle Paul is one of the greatest examples of what happens to a choleric when filled with the fruit of the Spirit. He went from being a powerful persecutor to a humble servant of God (Acts 8-9). Despite his strong personality, he always followed the direction of God. His choleric personality still reigned strong within him, but the Spirit of God now controlled him (Phil. 1:21-24). As you read about Paul's life you can see him growing stronger and stronger in the fruit of the Spirit. For example, as Paul and Barnabas were getting ready to leave for the second missionary journey they had a major disagreement about carrying John Mark (Acts 15:38). Barnabas wanted to carry him with them, but Paul was bitterly opposed to his presence because he had left them earlier (Acts 13:13). This argument ended with Paul and Barnabas separating. Yet, later on Paul would realize the worth of John Mark to his ministry (Col. 4:10; Phile. 1:24). On another occasion Paul had become impatient about this "thorn in the flesh" (1 Cor. 12:7-8), but grew in the Spirit of peace and patience through the grace of God.

THE PHLEGMATIC - The Peacemaker

JOY

The phlegmatic has a low-key personality that allows them to seemingly disappear in a room full of people. They are so quiet and still that you can forget they are there. Yet, as harmless as they may seem, Christians should be filled with a spirit of joy (*chara*). The Scriptures teach us, "*Whatever you do, work heartily, as for the Lord and not for men…*" (Col. 3:23). In other words, when we exhibit this attitude of working for God instead of men, the Spirit of joy will enter our hearts and remove the dread of work. Paul encouraged the Christians at Galatia "*to be made much of for a good purpose*" (Gal. 4:18). The problem with the church in Laodicea was their works were *neither cold nor hot* but *lukewarm* (Rev. 3:15-16). The phlegmatic has to be careful not to exhibit an unenthusiastic attitude.

FAITHFULNESS

One of the enduring qualities of the phlegmatic is a desire for peace. Their nature is to get along with everybody. In fact, they willingly follow the lead of others. This makes them great servants. However, the Christian realizes he cannot make everyone happy at the same time. There can be a problem of over commitment, which is the worst thing that can happen to a phlegmatic. They will not have the time or energy to complete the tasks and be seen by some as undependable.

The phlegmatic needs the Spirit of faithfulness (*pistis*), a trait that includes loyalty. Not just loyalty to Christians, but to Christ (1 Cor. 4:1-2). Sometimes you will have to disagree with your brothers (2 Tim. 4:3-5). The apostle Peter had to take a stand against the prejudice of the Jewish Christians (Acts 11:1-18). Priscilla and Aquila had to correct the outdated teachings of Apollos (Acts 18:24-26). The Corinthians had been set straight by Paul (1 and 2 Cor.). Timothy, our model phlegmatic, had to have the prodding of Paul to take a stand against the teachings of false doctrine (1 Tim. 1:3-10). Even Peter was confronted by Paul about his dealings with the Gentiles (Gal. 2:11-18).

PEACE

Although phlegmatics are known for peaceful attitude, they have a difficult struggle from within. Due to their overwhelming desire to be free of conflict they can tie themselves in knots working toward this end. The fact of the matter is: It doesn't matter how much we work at peace, there will always be difficulties to deal with in this world (Jn. 16:33). As soon as you smooth out one contention in your life, there is another that hits you from a different direction. Just as the melancholy gets depressed living in an imperfect world, the phlegmatic feels inner tension dwelling among people who do not always live for peace. In fact, some people strive for controversy, much like the choleric personality. This can be a real source of stress for those who do not like dissension.

Timothy seems to have had problems in this area, as we discussed in chapter four. There were many stressors in his life and he internalized his emotions. This may well be why Timothy had stomach problems (1 Tim. 5:23).

Timothy and all phlegmatic personalities need the *peace of God, which surpasses all understanding* to *guard your hearts and minds* (Phil. 4:7). The kind of peace the Spirit gives the Christian is an inner security, exactly what this type of personality needs. In fact, it is a trait that every temperament needs, and the only part of the fruit of the Spirit lacking in all four personalities. This is why Jesus said, *"Peace I leave with you; my peace I give to you. Not as the world gives do I give to you. Let not your hearts be troubled, neither let them be afraid"* (Jn. 14:27). What was this peace? The Holy Spirit Himself (v. 26).

God wants us to grow in the Fruit of the Spirit. He wants us to eliminate the weaknesses in our lives and develop the talents He blessed us with at birth. God can change you and make your life an *instrument of righteousness* (Rom. 6:13). The Word of God provides the anvil needed to mold the personality of the Christian and the Fruit of the Spirit becomes the hammer in the hands of the Carpenter to make us like Him.

Which fruits of the Spirit are your personality strengths? Which fruits are challenging within your personality? *"…love, joy, peace, patience, kindness, goodness, faithfulness, gentleness, self-control."*

CHAPTER 9

YIELD NOT TO TEMPTATION
What Leads You Into Temptation?

James 1:14 *"But each person is tempted when he is lured and enticed by his own desire."*

"Temptations from without have no power unless there is a corresponding desire from within." (E.C. McKenzie) All of us are enticed but not by the same desires. We all have different wants and needs. Ministers, elders, and therapists alike, counsel people for a number of things. There are those who would give up everything in their lives to have just a little bit more of what tempts them. Many of these are things I have never had the slightest desire to even try. It doesn't make me stronger or a better person, but it illustrates that temptations come from different desires. What tempts me and what tempts you are often different things/desires.

There are several factors that entice people to different stimulants. Gender, for example, is a cause of different fleshly urges. Typically, men are influenced more by sight and women more by the things they hear. A person's background is another factor. Studies show that a child raised in a home where abuse was present, has a greater chance of abusing their spouse or children than those who were not raised in that type of environment. So there are differences in temptation. Personality is another factor. In this study we have noted that each of us have varying strengths and weaknesses. Our temptations are linked to those flaws.

THE TEMPERAMENT TEMPTER

Satan is smart and he knows what entices us. He understands the personalities and their weaknesses and will use them to attack God's people. This goes all the way back to the beginning of man and woman in the Garden. The Scriptures say he is the most *subtle* (KJV), *crafty* (ESV), or *shrewdest* (NLT) of all of God's creation (Gen. 3:1). This was Satan's introduction to mankind. We have been warned. Peter wrote *"Be sober-minded; be watchful. Your adversary the devil prowls around like a roaring lion, seeking someone to devour"* (1 Pet. 5:8). His temptations are personal and sent out to us with our names attached to them.

We are given a glimpse of his wicked allurements with the first sin (Gen. 3:1-6). Satan attacked Eve in her moment of weakness. The text implies that she was thinking about the forbidden fruit. God simply said not to eat of the tree, but she talked about how God had said not to even touch it, which we have no record of Him saying (Gen. 2:17). Satan planted the temptation to fit her own personality weakness, and she ran with it.

WHAT LEADS *YOU* INTO TEMPTATION?

SANGUINE SEDUCTIONS (The Life of the Party)

TRYING TO PLEASE EVERYONE

The desire to please people is a Biblical principle (Rom. 15:1-3) but carried to extremes it becomes a weakness. The fact is it is impossible to please everyone. As the saying goes, "You can please some of the people all of the time, and all of the people some of the time, but you cannot please all of the people all of the time." The sanguine has such an intense desire to be popular it can eventually lead to sin.

We refer back to our prime sanguine example, the apostle Peter. In Galatians 2:11-16, Paul confronts Peter about violating the gospel of Christ. What was the violation? Peter was trying to please everyone. When he first came to Antioch he ate with the Gentile Christians (v. 12), but then was confronted by some of the Jewish friends of James about his association with these uncircumcised Gentiles. Being afraid of what these men might think, he stopped associating with the Gentile believers. It wasn't a fear for his life or freedom, because this wasn't an offense worthy of imprisonment or death. Peter was afraid of losing his popularity and prestige among the Jews. Peter was wrong and this is why Paul opposes him to his face for his actions.

This is why it is important for the sanguine to be dedicated to pleasing the Lord and not mankind. It is tempting to believe the opinions and traditions of well-known preachers and teachers of Christian universities, or the articles of popular brotherhood publications. Yet, we must seek the counsel of the Scriptures only, and not be afraid of the labeling and ridicule by others. The writer of Proverbs teaches us *"The fear of man lays a snare, but whoever trusts in the Lord is safe"* (Prov. 29:25).

PRONE TO EMOTIONALISM

No one can doubt the enthusiasm and energy the sanguine brings to the church. We are encouraged to have a zeal for the Lord (Col. 3:23; Gal. 4:18). However, there is the temptation to be over zealous and do things beyond the Scriptures. Emotionalism becomes a problem. Again, we need to be emotional and enthusiastic, but a sanguine can base everything on feelings. The Bible warns us about letting our feelings get out of hand. Paul penned *"...I bear them witness that they have a zeal for God, but not according to knowledge"* (Rom. 10:2). One translation calls it *misdirected zeal* (NLT). The Jews had a superficial religious knowledge but not the kind of knowledge that produced holiness. Outwardly they seemed very religious, but it wasn't based on God's Word. They lacked a correct understanding of what God wanted. This is the kind of danger the church has to beware of today. Being excited, changing up some old way of doing things, and promoting fresh ideas is only good if it doesn't violate God's Word.

CHOLERIC CRAVINGS (The Leader)

DOMINEERING OVER OTHERS

The choleric does not intend to dominate the people around them. They are successful in most of what they do and will try to help bring growth to the church. They realize God has blessed them with excellent leadership qualities, but Satan will try to use this against them.

Peter warned the elders not to become *"domineering over those in your charge"* (1 Pet. 5:3). This is a temptation for any choleric put into authority positions. This is why an elder must be controlled by the Spirit of God that made them overseers (Acts

20:28). The temptation is to abuse the power given by God. Jesus taught us leadership begins at the foot of the table and not the head (Jn. 13:1-17). This isn't to take away the authority elders possess or the submission of Christians to godly leadership (1 Tim. 5:1), but to properly govern it.

This allure of power and control is not limited to elders but any choleric Christian in the church. Diotrephes is the prime example of how this can effect the church. The apostle John described him as one *likes to put himself first, does not acknowledge our authority.* (2 Jn. 1:9) In other words, he likes being the leader. The temptation to dominate others leads to pride (1 Pet. 5:5), envy (Jms. 3:16), slander (Tit. 3:2), division (Jude 1:17-18), and rebellion (Rom. 13:2).

RELIANCE UPON SELF, NOT GOD

Because the cholerics are successful they are tempted to see themselves as the source of their accomplishments. The Lord blessed them with abilities to achieve, persevere, and lead. People often tell them how great they are or they may observe the lack of achievement from other temperaments in their field. They like the idea that they had the power to accomplish things without the help of others.

King David struggled with this temptation. On one occasion he conducted a census of Israel and Judah (2 Sam. 24). A census was basically a military draft, which seems harmless on the surface. However, the nation was at peace, so there was no need to enlist troops. Out of pride and ambition, David wanted this count so he could glory in the size of his army. He had put his faith in the size of his army rather than the Lord's ability to care for them. 2 Chronicles 21:1 is an interesting verse: *"Then Satan stood against Israel and incited David to number Israel."* Satan still tempts cholerics today to trust in themselves over God.

MELANCHOLY MAGNETISMS (The Perfectionist)

NEGATIVE THINKING

The Bible says our thoughts determine our actions (Prov. 4:23), and this principle is especially true for the melancholy. Negative thinking is the greatest temptation of this personality. There is a great battle that goes on within the mind (Rom. 7:23; 8:5-7). As Christians, we must fight this battle, but Satan knows this is one of the greatest battles for the melancholy.

There must be a new thought pattern to develop within the mind (Rom. 12:1-2). When we come to know the Lord our lives begin to change. It doesn't happen automatically. There is no button we push in the back of our heads that makes those negative thoughts and old habits go away. However, we are new creatures in Christ (2 Cor. 5:17), and now primarily the product of the work of Christ. Satan still tries to entice us into harmful thought patterns. He knows that if he can control our thoughts, he can control our actions.

Gideon shows what happens when we allow God to influence our minds. In Judges 6, the Midianites had conquered the Israelites because of their sinful behavior (v. 1). It was a bad situation, the people were hiding in caves and the enemy had destroyed their food supply (vv. 2-6). This was enough to cause the people to cry out for God's help. He heard them and selected a leader to bring them out – Gideon. Yet, Gideon did not see himself as someone who could lead this campaign, and he was pretty negative. *"And Gideon said to him, 'Please, sir, if the Lord is with us, why then has all this happened to us?...'"* (Jdg 6:13). This seemed pretty realistic. The angel of the Lord gave him further confidence but he could only reply, *"Please, Lord, how can I save Israel? Behold, my clan is the weakest in Manasseh, and I am the least in my father's house."* (Jdg. 6:15) Gideon could only see his limitations and weaknesses, rather than trusting God to work through him. God would soon turn this faltering attitude into faith. By the time the Lord finished with Gideon, he had enough faith to take an army of 300 to fight against the powerful Midian army of 135,000 fighting men (Jdg. 7-8).

Gideon was a great leader, but he was not a choleric. In fact, after this military crusade, the people asked him to be their leader. Here was his answer, *"I will not rule over you, and my son will not rule over you; the Lord will rule over you"* (Jdg. 8:23). Not the typical choleric leader response, even if he believed God was supreme. This shows how the Lord can work through the melancholy. Turn those negative thoughts into faith.

UNFORGIVING AND VENGEFUL

The introverted melancholy doesn't show vengeance the way the outspoken sanguine or choleric might, but can hold a grudge for years. This leads to an inner bitterness and lack of forgiveness. It works within the person. It is ungodly. Colossians 3:12-13 says, *"Put on then, as God's chosen ones, holy and beloved, compassionate hearts, kindness, humility, meekness, and patience, bearing with one another and, if one has a complaint against another, forgiving each other; as the Lord has forgiven you, so you also must forgive."* This why the melancholy must learn to deal with this temptation.

In the story of the prodigal son, the elder brother exemplifies the unforgiving spirit of this temperament (Lk. 15:11-32). Just like many melancholy children, he was the good son who always did what was asked of him. Yet, when his rebellious brother came home to a banquet, the older brother became upset and pouted. This was not the kind of outward anger commonly seen among the sanguine or choleric, but a quiet rebellion. The old brother simply would not go to the feast in his brothers honor (v. 28). He couldn't understand how his father could forgive so easily (v. 30). His unforgiving attitude robbed him of a joyful occasion.

This is a temptation of Satan. 2 Corinthians 2:10-11 *"Anyone whom you forgive, I also forgive. Indeed, what I have forgiven, if I have forgiven anything, has been for your sake in the presence of Christ, so that we would not be outwitted by Satan; for we are not ignorant of his designs."* To allow this attitude to continue is to fall into Satan's schemes.

PHLEGMATIC PLEASURES (The Peacemaker)

COMPROMISING THE TRUTH

This temptation stems from phlegmatic nature to keep the peace. Yet, there is no way to always be at peace in the world. There will always be conflict among personalities, people of different backgrounds, opinions, the rich and poor, the good and evil, etc. In a seminar I attended on *Conflict Resolution and Confrontation Skills* the speaker stated, "25% of people will like you regardless of what you say and do; 25% of people will not like you regardless of what you say and do; and 50% of the people do not have their minds made up yet." The point was, there is no way to please everyone. You can try, but it is impossible. There comes a time when you must take a stand for what you believe is right. For the phlegmatic, this can be difficult.

Abraham struggled with this idea. The Scriptures picture him as an easygoing and good-natured temperament. Yet, this easygoing nature caused him to compromise at times. On two occasions he asked his beautiful wife to lie about their relationship to keep him out of trouble (Gen. 12:10-13; 20:1-17). Later we see a man of faith who allowed God to take control instead of being controlled by his fears (Gen. 22:1-14).

There comes a time when every phlegmatic must take a stand for what is right, even knowing conflict will follow. You cannot always please God and mankind at the same time. There comes a time when a line must be drawn and one has to decide on which side of the line to stand. Abraham found out the hard way that straddling the fence causes greater pain than doing the right thing. This is why a strong faith in God is important in making the right decisions.

BEING STUBBORN

This is almost the exact opposite of someone who compromises, but a temptation of a phlegmatic. This personality doesn't like change and can stubbornly oppose it, especially if it involves too much work.

No one likes to be forced into doing something they do not want to do, even if it is for their own good. Proverbs 29:1 warns *"Whoever stubbornly refuses to accept criticism will suddenly be broken beyond repair"* (NLT). This is why the humble attitude of the phlegmatic must overcome the temptation to be stubborn.

All of us have temptations to conquer, and if we apply to our Christian lives the things we learned with the fruit of the Spirit (Gal. 5:22-23), we can prevail against the attacks of Satan. James tells us to *"resist the devil, and he will flee from you"* (Jms. 4:7).

WHAT LEADS YOU INTO TEMPTATION?

What temptations are hard for you? Trying to please everyone? Relying too much on emotions? Relying on self over Christ? Too much negative thinking? Being unforgiving and compromising the truth? Being stubborn?

CHAPTER 10

FINDING YOUR NICHE

Where do you belong in the Church?

As we have learned from our studies, the personalities form a wonderful group of diverse people with various abilities. All have specific strengths that are needed in the church. However, many times we do not know what to do with all these various temperaments. Sometimes we practically throw new Christians into whatever works we think of first without considering how they could use their talents most effectively for God. When there is a new program to get started, we generally go to one of the strongest members to take this work. The first, and sometimes only requirement, is their willingness to get involved. What about deacons? Most congregations find works that need to be overseen and appoint new deacons for those areas. Rather than matching the person to the work we usually say, "He seems like a good guy. He certainly matches up with the qualifications, so let's go with him." This doesn't mean those qualities are not important, but rarely do we set them up for success. When they fail it's too easy to label them as lazy, undependable, and are shocked because he had excelled in other things. The problem may have been the fact they were put in a position in which they were uncomfortable or unqualified.

If you need a strong leader for a certain work and you put a dominant phlegmatic over that work, you are setting them up for failure. If you need someone for a work that requires patience and is good with people, you do not need to put a choleric in charge. What about putting a true sanguine in a work that needs major organization skills? Then there are those areas that need high-energy personalities, but you put an introverted melancholy to get it done.

When Paul wrote to the Corinthian church, he urged them not to be ignorant concerning spiritual gifts and the placement of their people (1 Cor. 12:1). Yet, this is exactly the way congregations often go about their involvement ministries.

This chapter is intended to enlighten the church on the special gifts/abilities God has given every Christian through their personalities. While there is a difference in the spiritual gifts of 1 Corinthians 12 and the natural abilities of our personalities, there are many similarities. The Holy Spirit does help us strengthen our personality and character as we cultivate His fruit in our lives.

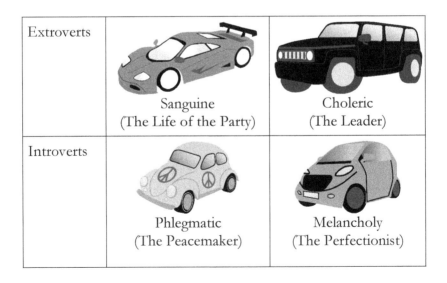

Extroverts	Sanguine (The Life of the Party)	Choleric (The Leader)
Introverts	Phlegmatic (The Peacemaker)	Melancholy (The Perfectionist)

EVERY PERSONALITY HAS GIFTS

In 1 Corinthians 12:7, Paul says *"To each is given the manifestation of the Spirit."* God gave each one spiritual gifts for the use of His service in the Kingdom of God, just as every one of us have personality strengths to use to God's glory. Each one of us should be thankful for those gifts. Every ability you have is from God. Every good gift is from Him (James 1:17).

One of the problems with Corinthian church was their discontentment with spiritual gifts (vv. 15-16). Some of them wanted the showy, popular, or powerful gifts, as opposed to the more hidden or unattractive gifts of God. This was arrogance as God has placed each one of us *as he chose* (v. 18). This questions God's wisdom and goodness by implying He made a mistake. Our natural personalities are exactly what they are supposed to be. Later we will talk about "masking" our personalities.

EACH PERSONALITY HAS DIFFERENT GIFTS

1 Corinthians 12:4-6 *"Now there are varieties of gifts, but the same Spirit; and there are varieties of service, but the same Lord; and there are varieties of activities, but it is the same God who empowers them all in everyone."*

God blesses His church with many different gifts. This is easily seen in the temperaments. Look at all the ways God has blessed each personality for the Lord's service. There is no doubt in my mind that God planned to give us the four personality types to do Christ's work and glorify God.

Let's think about this for a moment. What would it be like if everyone had the same personality? If all the church were sanguine (Life of the Party) then no one could get a word in edge-wise. They wouldn't have anyone to listen to them because each one would be trying to get their own audience to listen.

What if the church was made up of all cholerics (Leaders)? We would never lack for leaders, but they could never be effective without having someone to follow them. There would be more splits in the church than already occur, that is for certain. Think about a whole church full of Diotrephes' (3 Jn. 9)!

As perfect and talented a group as the melancholy (Perfectionist) may be, how would they decide on the proper form of organization? Even if they did, nothing would get done because everything would be over analyzed and criticized to death.

At least with a world filled with phlegmatics (Peacemaker) we would finally have world peace, but our churches would become obsolete because no one would be willing to speak publicly, and besides, everyone could stay at home and "do church" on their own.

Here is what Paul said, *"If the whole body were an eye, where would be the sense of hearing? If the whole body were an ear, where would be the sense of smell?"*

Diversity is good. In fact, Paul said that diversity actually brings unity in the body of Christ (v. 12, 20), using the human body to illustrate his point. The body is a complex system that works together. We unify because we realize how much we need each other. As much as the sanguine drives the melancholy nuts, they will admit they are good to have around when they need cheering up. On the flip side, as much as the melancholy nags the sanguine about their disorganization, they are glad to have them when they start looking for things in the teacher supply room. The choleric may seem bossy to phlegmatic, but they are nice to have around when you need someone to make an important decision for the church. The phlegmatic may not move as fast as a choleric would like, but their calming presence is nice when things seem to get out of hand.

The personalities cannot function without each other. They make our ministries complete, and once we realize this, we will have a greater appreciation for one another.

We are different, but we are all equally important. Paul wrote *"The eye cannot say to the hand, 'I have no need of you,' nor again the head to the feet, 'I have no need of you.' On the contrary, the parts of the body that seem to be weaker are indispensable, and on those parts of the body that we think less honorable we bestow the greater honor, and our unpresentable parts are treated with greater modesty, which our more presentable parts do not require. But God has so composed the body, giving greater honor to the part that lacked it, that there may be no division in the body, but that the members may have the same care for one another. If one member suffers, all suffer together; if one member is honor, all rejoice together"* (vv. 21-26). Some of the more gifted members felt they were more important and could live without the help of these *weaker* or *less honorable* Christians. Paul is referring to the parts of the body that are less showy, at least it seems that way. In reality these parts are just as important. Paul says they are needed. Every personality has gifts that are necessary for the other temperaments in the church, and it would be wrong for one personality to think they are more vital than another.

EVERY PERSONALITY IS TO USE THEIR GIFTS

Our temperament strengths are tools for God to use for service. Before we became Christians our abilities were used for selfish reasons, such as, to excel in business, to be popular, or make good grades. Yet, when we are born again, we change from a life of the flesh to a life of submission to Christ (Rom. 6:4-7; 2 Cor. 5:12-21). To use our abilities for self and not for God would be sinful. Our blessings are on loan from God, and we are told to be good stewards of these things (1 Pet. 4:10). And while God gives these blessings to us, we are to use them to serve Him and others.

A sanguine that doesn't use their enthusiasm to edify the church (1 Thess. 5:11), fails to use their talents for Christ. A choleric that only uses their leadership abilities to build a great business, but never builds up the church (Rom. 2:5-11), will never fulfill their greatest accomplishments in life. A melancholy that allows their introverted personality to keep them from sharing their genius to discern the Scriptures with others wastes one of the greatest gifts in the church (I Cor. 14:19). And the phlegmatic that withholds his ability to bring peace and harmony among his fellow Christians (Matt. 5:9), may allow the greatest tragedy of all – division.

A moment ago we noticed why it would be wrong for one Christian to say, "I have no need of you" (v. 21) to the other gifts in the church. However, it would equally be wrong for a believer to say, "They don't need me." Listen to what Paul states in verses 15 and 16 *"If the foot should say, 'Because I am not a hand, I do not belong to the body,' that would not make it any less a part of the body. And if the ear should say, 'Because I am not an eye, I do not belong to the body,' that would not make it any less a part of the body."* Some of the Christians thought their gifts were less important. This is the same thing that can happen among the personalities.

Every one of us is dependent upon the other. We are all unique and God needs each of us using our gifts. When we don't, we let God down as well as the body of believers. It isn't fair to ask a sanguine to organize a program of the church, just because they come up with the idea. Nor is it fair to ask the melancholy to promote the works they organize. To put a phlegmatic as the leader because no one else will step up is dangerous. And to ask a choleric to work on a project that demands great patience would be like setting a bull loose in a china shop. The hand needs the eye to focus on the object it is about to use. The hands need the legs to carry it to the place it needs to work. Everyone is needed within the church.

USING YOUR PERSONALITY FOR CHRIST

1 Corinthians 12 gives a list of spiritual gifts, some were temporary and others are relevant today. We will be focusing on these gifts that also relate to our personalities.

1 Corinthians 12:8-11 *"For to one is given through the Spirit the utterance of wisdom, and to another the utterance of knowledge according to the Spirit, to another faith by the same Spirit, to another gifts of healing by the one Spirit, to another the working of miracles, to another prophecy, to another the ability to distinguish between spirits, to another various kinds of tongues, to another the interpretation of tongues. All these are empowered by one and the same Spirit, who apportions to each one individually as he wills."*

1 Corinthians 12:28 *"And God appointed in the church first apostles, second prophets, third teachers, then miracles, then gifts of healing, helping, administrating, and various kinds of tongues."*

GIFTS OF THE SANGUINE (The Life of the Party)
Utterance of wisdom (v. 8). Utterance indicates the ability to speak. This would certainly fall under the strengths of a sanguine. This personality is a great communicator and can bring powerful messages of God's Word. These are preachers and Bible class teachers who use hand motions, facial expressions, and powerful visual aids.

Prophecy (v. 10). When we think of prophecy, we think of telling the future (13:8). However, the Greek word (*propheteuo*) can also mean, "to declare truths." This refers to public speaking. Actually, the suggestion of predictions of the future was added sometime in the Middle Ages. This is not to say prophets did not foretell the future, but this wasn't their basic mission. Speaking before others is a sanguine strength.

Teachers (v. 28). The word *teachers* (*didaskalos*) give the idea of studying and expounding God's Word to the church. Actually, these were the men who encouraged and instructed the new converts taught by the evangelists. I guess we call these "new convert classes" today. It takes a special teacher to impart knowledge to a group of people who know almost nothing about being a Christian. This is a much needed and important gift in the church. The sanguine would be interesting, easy to get to know, and enthusiastic in this role.

GIFTS OF THE CHOLERIC (The Leader)

Administrating (v. 28). If there is one spiritual gift that sums up the personality strength of the choleric, this is it. This is an interesting word (*kubernesis*), which means "dictatorship." Now I really have the choleric' attention. William Barclay points out that this word "literally refers to the work of a pilot who steers the ship through the rocks and shoals to harbour." This has to do with one who has the talent to keep the church on course. They are able to make quick and wise decisions. They will circle the church up, motivate them, and then direct them toward the goal. If you find a choleric controlled by the Spirit of God they can accomplish amazing things for the Lord. They must continue to tell themselves that they are the pilot and not the owner of the ship. This was a gift that was not being used in the Corinthian church (1 Cor. 14:40), or at best rejected by others. But Paul helped them to see the necessity of this gift.

GIFTS OF THE MELANCHOLY (The Perfectionist)

Utterance of knowledge (v. 8). The gift of *knowledge* (*gnosis*) is the ability to perceive, learn, and recognize God's Word. It is the ability to understand the mysteries of the Bible. Some in the first century were given supernatural abilities to do this (Rom. 16:25-26). This seems to have been the case in Corinth (1 Cor. 2:6-16). Today God still gives Christians the ability to uncover the truths found in the Scriptures. One special means is through personalities like the melancholy who is gifted in the field of research and discovery. They are our writers of commentaries, Bible class materials, and other reference books. This knowledge helps the church to understand God's message to a higher degree.

Distinguishing between spirits (v. 10). This *distinguishing (diakrisis)* refers to one who has the ability to separate or distinguish one from another. In the time of the New Testament, as today, there were false prophets and teachers. Simon the Sorcerer used magic to make others believe he possessed the power of God (Acts. 8:10). Jesus warned us to beware of false prophets (Matt. 7:15; 24:11,24), as did Paul (2 Cor. 11:13), and John (1 Jn. 4:1-3). Peter devoted a whole chapter on it in 2 Peter 2, and Jude would dedicate an entire letter dealing with its dangers. The melancholy possesses a great non-miraculous ability to *"examine the Scriptures daily to see if these things were so"* (Acts 17:11). This is greatly needed in the church today. Our world is filled with thousands of religions, all teaching something different from the other. Even within the churches of Christ you find various views on what is right and wrong. Satan is still the *father of lies* (Jn. 8:44), and does everything he can to confuse the Good News of Jesus (Mk. 4:14-15; 2 Cor. 4:3-4). We need those who can study and analyze the Scriptures, and the melancholy excels in this gift.

Teachers (v. 28). Along with the sanguine and his ability to communicate, the melancholy has the ability to study and interpret. This gift isn't so much in the area of speaking ability, as it was the understanding, explaining and interpreting the Scriptures.

GIFTS OF THE PHLEGMATIC (The Peacemaker)

Faith (v. 9). The gift of *faith (pistis)* goes much deeper than saving faith. It is fully trusting God in the most difficult of times, like the faith of the mustard seed (Matt. 17:20). This is the kind of faith that remains calm in the face of terrible storms. No personality displays this strength as well as the phlegmatic. Whether we realize it or not, it is a powerful gift in the church. It encourages others to be courageous. We are strengthened when we learn of fellow disciples who displayed an unshakeable faith in tough times. That is what the phlegmatic can bring to the church.

Helping (v. 28). This is a beautiful word (*antilempsis*) that describes something that is given in exchange for another. As used in this context, it is taking the burden off another and placing it upon ourselves. These are people who helped and supported the poor, the sick, disabled, widows, and orphans. These are the gentle people who have a heart for the weak (Acts 20:35). While not a showy gift it is an essential one (Phil. 2:25, 30).

These are only a few of the many ways each personality type can use their strengths to serve the church. Our next point will expound further.

WHERE DO YOU BELONG IN THE CHURCH?

WHERE DOES THE SANGUINE FIT? I would love to take all the dominant sanguines in the church, once a year, and brainstorm for ideas. No doubt many of these could never be used, or might be impossible at the time, but you would be surprised how many of these would aid the church. These temperaments are excellent at visiting, edifying others, helping with the youth program, fellowship, etc.

Suggested or possible areas of service: Leading prayers, teaching (especially children and teens), speaking, making announcements, greeting visitors, visitation, hosting church activities, advertising, decorating, etc.

WHERE DOES THE MELANCHOLY FIT? After I receive all the ideas from the sanguine crowd, I would take them over to the melancholy group. They would determine which ones could be used and organize these ideas to accomplish the task. They could even use their famous pie charts and graphs.

Suggested or possible areas of service: teaching (especially adult classes), organizing activities, special days, mission works, etc., serving as church treasurer, doing clerical work, making repairs, creating bulletin boards, painting murals, maintaining the church library, etc.

WHERE DOES THE CHOLERIC FIT? Now that certain works have been decided upon and organized, I would hand these over to the choleric group so they could discover which one could lead the new programs. From there they would recruit the help they needed to get to work. They could utilize the sanguine to help advertise and get others excited about the work.

Suggested or possible areas of service: leading prayers, teaching, speaking, directing programs, supervising, training teachers, leading mission trips, etc.

WHERE DOES THE PHLEGMATIC FIT? The new ideas have been organized and are ready to be implemented, but before that happens I would want to go through one more personality group – phlegmatic. They will give the added compassion and love that is needed for every work of the church. Can you imagine having a benevolence program without compassion (Matt. 25:31-46), or conducting an evangelistic work without love (Eph. 4:15)? Not only that, but also this personality will help all the other temperaments unite and work these programs in peace.

Suggested or possible areas of service: preparing the Lord's Supper, serving communion to shut-ins, writing letters of encouragement, helping in the nursery, preparing food for those hurting, etc.

Every personality has a place in the church. I hope this helps you as you find your niche among the Lord's work

CHAPTER 11

A MODERN DAY "MIRACLE"

Getting Along with Difficult Christians

I have been in church work long enough to know there are some Christians (I use the term loosely) who are very difficult to get along with on a daily basis. You may be thinking they are only in the congregation you serve, but I am here to tell you they are everywhere. Sometimes preachers (or members) have a bad encounter with a fellow member, and believe leaving is the best option. Granted, there are some congregations that have more difficult members than others, but difficult people are in every church around the world. Why? Because the church is made up of varying personalities, with all their strengths and weaknesses.

One of the definitions of the word *difficult* is "hard to understand." It is a person who acts in opposition to another. They are difficult because they are not like you, made up of varying strengths and certain weaknesses. Yet, the question remains, "Can we get along with difficult people in the church?" What if those people are elders, deacons, or a minister? Can we really learn to get along? I'm not advocating these people will become our best friends (not that it is impossible). Nor am I saying you will always be able to get along with every member of the church. There are some things that must always be considered:

- Some people are mentally incapable of getting along with others. This may be due to some psychosomatic disorder. There may be things in their past that need to be dealt with to have healthy relationships. In some cases, the negative reactions of others cannot be helped.

- Some people are unwilling to get along with others. They could care less about doing the will of God, and especially about their fellow man. For them "Church" is a political move, or just something they were "forced" to do growing up. This is really unfortunate.

- 25%, 25%, 50% rule - remember?

Hopefully you have already learned to appreciate the various temperaments in the church. This knowledge will go a long way toward congregational unity and tolerance. This chapter is designed to enhance your knowledge and give you the skills needed in dealing with those difficult Christians in the church.

If this lesson can prevent one congregation from splitting or one relationship ending it will have been worth all the time and research of this book. Let's face it, most church divisions are personality-related issues and not doctrinal stands.

WHO ARE THESE DIFFICULT PEOPLE?

The first thing we must do is have an understanding of the different kinds of Christians is to know the things you can expect from certain personality types. These may be the things that bother others in the church, and are important for us to recognize in order to get along with them.

SANGUINE CHRISTIANS - Life of the Party

They act like children. One author calls them "bigger children." They leave their toys lying all around the house and have to be told to clean up. Especially if they ever borrow a projector from the teacher supply room, books from the church library, or a stapler from the secretary. The other personalities look at their disorganization as rude and inconsiderate.

Also, like a child, they look for the shiny new quarter in every work. If it's not fun, then they believe it is their responsibility to "revive the program." But their shenanigans can be annoying during meetings, especially if you are the target of their jokes. The more sensitive temperaments find this irritating.

The sanguine likes to quote Jesus' statement to *"become like children"* (Matt. 18:3), while the other temperaments quote Paul who said, *"When I was a child, I spoke like a child, I thought like a child, I reasoned like a child. When I became a man I gave up childish ways"* (1 Cor. 13:11). As much as we want the sanguine to grow up, it is highly unlikely, so we must learn to get along.

They talk faster than they think. Actually it might be more fitting to say they talk and don't think at all. They make remarks that appear insensitive, and are made at inappropriate times. The deep thinking melancholy, who always thinks before speaking, believes this shortcoming is inexcusable. I wonder what the other apostles were thinking when Peter started to sink into the Sea of Galilee. Do you think Peter's brother and friends rolled their eyes and whispered to themselves, "Here we go again," as he began to sink? This was not the first time Peter had acted without thinking, nor would it be his last. Plus Peter made the others look bad volunteering to jump into the raging sea. We know there was a battle between them over who was the greatest (Mk. 9:33-34). Peter sank because he had no depth. This really aggravates the thinker.

This is not an exhaustive list but gives you a good idea of the type of sanguine traits that aggravate us.

CHOLERIC CHRISTIANS - The Leader

They hurt the feelings of others. It's not that they mean to come across as cold and callused, they just say what is going through their minds at the moment. They just tell people how they feel, even if it is about you. This is how they want you to treat them. This is totally different from the melancholy and phlegmatic who think before speaking.

For example, someone comes up with the idea of having a get together for their Bible class group. The discussion turns to food; a melancholy finally speaks up (after careful thought) and gives a detailed menu of the perfect meal. They even start a well-organized list for people to sign up for the items needed, including a section for diet drinks and cocktail napkins. But then it happens, the plainspoken choleric speaks up and says, "I don't like that kind of meal." Maybe it was the sanguine who had come up with an exciting theme for the evening when another choleric says, "That sounds stupid." The next thing you know the class decides not to have a party and people leave that morning angry, that is, except the choleric. They think everything is fine and are wondering why everyone decided not to get together. They did not mean to make everyone upset.

They are aggressive. This goes along with their leadership temperament. Sometimes they can be pushy and demanding, all the things the phlegmatic hates in leadership. Therefore, there can be some real conflict between these two temperament types. Also, their blunt speech creates a wall between them and the melancholy. Even the sanguine can become offended if their feelings are not considered.

Have you ever encountered this personality in the church? These are the "church growth experts" who drive, push, and sometimes yell to get people do do what they believe is the way to growth. Whether we like it or not, though, they usually are right! But putting up with their abuse can be wearing. They don't mean to make people mad, they are only determined to be successful. When we incur their wrath it is only because we are in their path to succeed. It wasn't that they had a problem with you personally. The problem is most people do not like to be pushed. It can be very difficult for this personality to separate their worldly business with the Lord's business. The problem being, Christians are not paid to work for the choleric, they work for God (Matt. 5:16). Cholerics mean well, but come across too strong. This sounds a lot like the choleric apostle Paul and his dealings with Barnabas (Acts 15:36-41).

MELANCHOLY CHRISTIANS - The Perfectionist

They are negative thinkers. They are the geniuses of the personalities, and therefore logically calculate every work in the church. This is good and needed in the church, but will sometimes leave no room for faith in their figures and pie charts. The melancholy mind works in problem solving and will many times forecast future problems that can be avoided. But, when carried to extremes, they will leave out the most important component in church work – faith and providence. These things cannot be calculated on a piece of paper or tabulated on the most sophisticated computer software. This is why the sanguine gets upset when their great ideas are shot down by well-meaning melancholies who insist, "It's not in the budget," or "we have never done it that way before." Common sense is needed before carrying out a work, but so is the faith in *things not seen* (Heb. 11:1). Melancholy members don't mean to be negative and feel they are just being realistic.

They get their feelings hurt. It is hard for the choleric to understand feelings, but for the deep thinking melancholy it is a part of their everyday life. This is good and needed in the church, especially when dealing with other people. However, because they are intense thinkers, they can over analyze comments or actions of other Christians. Someone can approach a melancholy during a fellowship meal and really brag on how good their dish looked. Maybe it was the way they organized a fruit tray, or how their meringue turned out on their pie, but to them they begin to wonder if they were saying it didn't taste good. Why? Because they only commented on how good it looked. They begin to think, "Maybe that was their way of saying it didn't taste good." The rest of the afternoon they think about that comment and become further convinced this was their intent. By Sunday night they won't even talk to them because of the rude comment they made about their food. A sensitive melancholy can put themselves and those around them through a lot of pain.

PHLEGMATIC CHRISTIANS - The Peacemaker

They would rather not get involved. It isn't that they don't care about the church and its growth; they see involvement as potential controversy. I knew someone who passed up an opportunity to lead a mission trip because they didn't want to deal with all the potential arguments. They would be more than willing to assist, but didn't really want to find themselves in the middle of a conflict. As mentioned before, this seems to have been the mindset of Timothy (1 Tim. 1:3). For the choleric leader, this can be difficult to understand. They do not like conflict either, but they realize it is sometimes necessary in order to reach the ultimate goal. The phlegmatic Christian appears, at least to them, as if they don't care about the glory of God. It can be frustrating to the choleric who has made many sacrifices for Christ.

They do not get overly excited. I did not say they are incapable of enthusiasm, only that they do not show passion. The phlegmatic is the most mellow and least excitable of all the temperaments. For the sanguine (life of the party), this can be disappointing, especially when they have been personally involved. There have been times I have been excited about certain things I witnessed on a given Sunday (visitors, baptisms, restorations, people getting involved, etc.), and begin to share my joy with fellow Christians. But occasionally you run across someone who isn't quite excited, at least outwardly. As a sanguine you want to shake them and say, "Did you hear what I said?" Yet, the sooner we learn the phlegmatic doesn't jump for joy, we can better understand why we have a difficult time relating.

Have you ever met these personalities in the church? Some of you had a face and name in mind as you read about these difficult personalities.

DEALING WITH DIFFICULT CHRISTIANS

Now that we have a better understanding of why people seem to be difficult, it is important to understand some ways we can better get along.

Paul told the Christians at Colosse, *"Put on then, as God's chosen ones, holy and beloved, compassionate hearts, kindness, humility, meekness, and patience, bearing with one another and, if one has a complaint against another, forgiving each other; as the Lord has forgiven you, so you also must forgive"* (Col. 3:12-13). The church must look past the weaknesses of their fellow Christians and seek understanding. When Paul was dealing with the conflict between Euodia and Syntyche, he was dealing with personality conflict, in that he did not take sides (Phil. 4:2-3). His plea was for them to settle their dispute. When you learn to deal with the difficult people in your life, it will result in great blessings for the church (Ps. 133).

SAM AND SAMANTHA SANGUINE – Praise
The one thing a sanguine desires more than the other temperaments is recognition. Some call it egotistical, but the Bible refers to it as brotherhood (Prov. 12:25). We are not talking about false flattery (Prov. 28:23), but genuine recognition. There are many positive traits the sanguine offers the church – energy, enthusiasm, creativity, friendliness, etc. When used in the proper way, it can go a long way in communicating, even in difficult situations. Paul used this approach on Philemon before he discussed the difficult matter of his runaway slave, Onesimus (Phile. 1:1-7), as did Christ in dealing with the churches of Asia (Rev. 2:2-6; 13-16; 19-20).

Our sanguine, Peter, had this need for praise. After Jesus told the rich young ruler to give up his life to follow Him, the young man went away sad, because he wasn't willing to make that type of commitment. However, Peter spoke up and reminded Christ that he and the other disciples made that decision and basically asked, "What's our reward?" (Matt. 19:27). Jesus did not scold Peter for his selfish question, but actually assured him that they would receive a hundred times as much in heaven (v. 28-29). Jesus must have recognized Peter's need for praise. He had already demonstrated his willingness to follow Christ on the stormy seas of Galilee, even though it ended in failure. Yet, Jesus knew Peter needed encouragement, and provided some for him (Matt. 16:17-19). It was right after this the Lord had to rebuke Peter for standing in the way of God's plans (v. 21-23). Peter listened because Christ provided him with the things his personality needed, and became one of the great men of faith.

Sanguines need encouragement and appreciation. They are emotional people who need to know you care. When given the right amount of encouragement and in the right way you will be surprised how well you will get along.

CHRIS AND CHRISTY CHOLERIC – Power
Born leaders, like the choleric, need to be in control. Why not? They are the most dependable, decisive, and determined of all the personalities. That would be fine for most people, but following them can be difficult. Making them feel like they are in control is the key to getting along. I did not say to let them run over you, in fact, the choleric respects the person who will take a stand. The important thing to remember is not to make them feel like their authority is in jeopardy. How do you do that? Help them understand you are trying to do what is best in accomplishing their mission, not that you think it should be aborted. A choleric wants their works to succeed and if you can help them understand why you differ they will change. Not only that, but they will have a newfound respect for you and your opinions.

Barnabas knew what it was like to work with a controlling choleric in the church. The Apostle Paul would have been difficult to work with at times. He was very demanding and determined, both before and after his conversion. No one can deny his success, establishing churches all over Asia and Greece on three missionary journeys. But Barnabas knew how to deal with him. Paul always knew Barnabas was on his side, since the very beginning (Acts 9:26-28), and never tried to rebel against his mission. Oh yes, Barnabas had words with Paul (Acts 15:36-39), but he never tried to sabotage the mission. He never threatened his authority. In fact, Barnabas still helped Paul complete his work; they just took different directions. You don't find Barnabas telling the church that Paul needed to be relieved of his duties or that he was going to take his ball and go home. Barnabas selected another partner and continued the work. They agreed to disagree and let God's work continue. Their friendship continued as Paul made favorable mention of Barnabas (and John Mark) in his letters (1 Cor. 9:6; Col. 4:10).

No one said getting along with a choleric would be easy, but it is not impossible. In fact, having a friend like the choleric has its benefits – they will always stand up for you when others bring you down, and usually have political power to help you later.

MELVIN AND MELISSA MELANCHOLY – Preparation

It had to be a melancholy who came up with the "Schedule of Worship" found in most Sunday morning bulletins. No doubt the traditional three songs and a prayer originated with this temperament, and once the other melancholy Christians heard about this organized system, it became a law. I do believe there is a need for some kind of order so everyone isn't speaking at the same time, but to make a "Schedule of Worship" law would be wrong. The melancholy needs this structure in their lives and demand it (in a subtle way). If you want to get along with this type personality, then you must learn to give attention to details.

For example, if you go into a room with melancholy elders and say, "This church needs to start evangelizing the community. I want to make an announcement, for anyone interested, to meet in the church parking lot on Saturdays." I can already hear the questions, "What time will you begin and end? Will everyone walk, ride in cars (who drives?), or use bicycles (what if someone doesn't have a bike?)? What if there is bad weather? Who's going to be in charge? Who's going to decide where everyone goes and keep up with where they have been? How will we know which houses have been contacted and which ones were not at home? Will the group pass out tracts or brochures about the church? Is the intent to invite them to services or ask for a Bible study? What kind of Bible study program would you use? Will this include children? Etc., etc., etc." For the good-hearted sanguine who came up with the idea, they can take this line of questioning to mean "the elders are not serious about soul winning." When in reality they are trying to figure out the best way to accomplish the task.

Moses was a true melancholy. In Exodus 18, we find a potential dispute between Moses and his father-in-law Jethro. The Israelites had just been freed from Egyptian bondage (Ex. 13:17-22), and won a difficult battle with the Amalekites (Ex. 17:8-16). Moses has just been reunited with his family, from whom he could have been separated for up to a year. They had not departed on the best of terms and the text may indicate it was still a sensitive situation. Jethro observed that Moses was overworked. How would his father-in-law tell him he is a workaholic? Questioning Moses' organization skills could lead to strife, especially for a melancholy. Jethro appealed to his temperament by laying out a detailed plan (Ex. 18:21-22 – judges over 1000, 100, 50, and 10), as well as using logic (v. 23 – ask God). The end result, *"Moses listened to the voice of his father-in-law and did all that he had said"* (v. 24). This advice is still being used by melancholies around the world. Jethro gave Moses order in his life.

PHIL AND PHYLLIS PHLEGMATIC – Peace
The phlegmatic Christian is someone who has one simple goal – to get along with others. When this principle is threatened they can climb into a shell and distance themselves from the rest of the church. Communication becomes impossible, involvement will be non-existent, and the threat of leaving will always be on their minds. So the question is, how do you deal with a personality that can get their feelings hurt easily? There are times, out of ignorance, that they will do things that are not right. At times, especially in matters of opinion, you can let it go, but other times something has to be said.

It is important to note that the phlegmatic doesn't work well with sarcasm or rudeness. No one likes to be dealt with in this way, but especially the phlegmatic, and no one can expect them to "toughen their skin" like the choleric. This personality is made to function differently. They do work well with compromise, diplomacy, and sincerity. It is important to build a safe environment that would soften the fears and concerns of the other. Give them reassurance and praise, without compromising the issues at hand. This will help set the proper setting in dealing with their problems. Solomon said, *"a soft tongue will break a bone"* (Prov. 25:15).

We again turn to the example of how choleric Paul dealt with phlegmatic Timothy. Paul knew of his tendencies to be timid (2 Tim. 1:7-8). Yet, unlike the "sharp" dispute he had with Barnabas, Paul was much kinder to his phlegmatic friend Timothy. Using a more diplomatic approach rather than the "in-your-face" tactic used at times. Paul tries to motivate Timothy (1 Tim. 1:18), using persuasive works of encouragement (1 Tim. 6:11-20), and appealing to his gifts (1 Tim. 6:12-15; 2 Tim. 1:6). In turn, they had a great relationship, as Paul referred to Timothy as his *true child in the faith"* (1 Tim. 1:2).

To get along with Phil and Phyllis Phlegmatic, you must learn to be sensitive to their needs. Offer help, clarify problems, strengthen your relationships, and build them up.

HOW DIFFICULT PEOPLE VIEW YOU

Maybe you heard about the young man who was a new student from Scotland. The fact that he had made it into the prestigious Oxford University and his clan was very proud. However, they wondered how he would make it going to school in another land. After the first month, his mother came to visit. She asked him how he had gotten along with the English students. He said, "Mother, they're such terrible, noisy people. The one on that side keeps banging his head against the wall, and won't stop. The one on the other side screams and screams and screams, away into the night." His mother asked him how he had managed to put up with such noisy neighbors. He said, "Mother, I do nothing. I just ignore them. I just stay here quietly, playing my bagpipes."

The point is: sometimes those difficult people in our lives are the very ones who find us irritating (and perhaps for a better reason). You ask any personality who they find annoying and they will say in essence, "everyone else except my personality." It is hard to see ourselves as the problem in a relationship, because it seems so normal and right. That is why it is important to look at ourselves first, to see if we are the ones causing the problems around us. Solomon said *"If you shout a pleasant greeting to your neighbor too early in the morning, it will be counted as a curse!"* (Prov. 27:14 – NLT).

You can get along with difficult people, with the proper patience and understanding. No one said it would be easy, only that it can be done. I cannot stress the importance of this lesson with the church. Getting along with our brethren is of the utmost importance. I pray that this chapter will help your relationships in the church.

ABOUT THE AUTHOR

Tracy Moore was born and raised in Hamilton, Alabama. He has been married 23 years to Melissa Webster. They have four children – Lex (21), Noah (18), Micah (14), and Bella (10), as well a spoiled dog named Max. Tracy has been in ministry 23 years. He is currently the pulpit minister in Vero Beach, Florida. He received a Bible degree from Faulkner University and a Master's degree in Christian Counseling from Christian Bible College and Seminary.

Along with his local ministry, he conducts seminars around the southeast United States on personalities and the church. Tracy is actively involved with the preachers and churches of the Caribbean.

In his free time, Tracy loves spending time with his family, fishing, trying weird foods, watching his favorite sports teams (Roll Tide!), playing basketball, and reading up on World War II history.

You can learn more about Tracy's work in personality studies at http://www.personalitychurch.com. For seminars or other events contact Tracy at tracylmoore@msn.com.

CPSIA information can be obtained
at www.ICGtesting.com
Printed in the USA
BVHW040220241218
536319BV00015B/269/P

9 781500 463106